THE BRISTOL EXPERIENCE

A personal assessment of the unique life-enhancing programme for cancer patients and carers

Liz Hodgkinson and Jane Metcalfe

VERMILION
LONDON

1 3 5 7 9 10 8 6 4 2

Text copyright © Liz Hodgkinson & Jane Metcalfe 1995

The right of Liz Hodgkinson & Jane Metcalfe to be identified as the authors of
this book has been asserted by them in accordance with the Copyright,
Designs & Patents Act, 1988.

First published in the United Kingdom in 1995 by
Vermilion
an imprint of Ebury Press
Random House
20 Vauxhall Bridge Road
London SW1V 2SA

Random House Australia (Pty) Limited
20 Alfred Street, Milsons Point, Sydney,
New South Wales 2061, Australia

Random House New Zealand Limited
18 Poland Road, Glenfield,
Auckland 10, New Zealand

Random House South Africa (Pty) Limited
PO Box 337, Bergvlei, South Africa

Random House Canada
1265 Aerowood Drive, Mississauga,
Ontario L4W 1B9, Canada

Random House UK Limited Reg. No. 954009

A CIP catalogue record for this book is available
from the British Library.

0 09 178980 X

Typeset by Deltatype Ltd, Ellesmere Port, Wirral
Printed and bound in Great Britain by Mackays of Chatham plc, Chatham, Kent

Papers used by Ebury Press are natural recyclable products
made from wood grown in sustainable forests.

'You cannot discover new oceans unless you have the courage to lose sight of the shore'

Manny Patel

Acknowledgements

The idea behind this book was to present an objective, jargon-free and accessible description of the Bristol Cancer Help Centre, aimed particularly at those who may have considered the Centre's work to be too 'way out' for them. For this reason it was essential to write the book from an outsider's point of view. Liz Hodgkinson, who has a wealth of writing experience in the field of complementary medicine, was the ideal candidate for such a venture. The first half of the book is therefore her perspective on the Centre, and the remainder is a synthesis of joint experiences.

I would like to thank the following for their support, help and advice: all the staff of the Bristol Cancer Help Centre, particularly Wanda Nowak, Pat Pilkington and Dr Rosy Daniel; former patients who have generously and courageously contributed aspects of their cancer journeys; and special thanks to Heather Goodare, Jane Warren and Michael Stuart.

Jane Metcalfe
August 1994

Contents

Introduction   ix

Part One

1 The Bristol Experience   3
2 The Early Days   21
3 Scandal!   32
4 Bristol After Chilvers   43

Part Two – The Bristol Therapies

Introduction   55
5 Nutrition   59
6 Bristol Recipes   70
7 Visualisation   74
8 Breathing and Relaxation   80
9 Hands-on Therapies: Massage and Shiatsu   87
10 Music and Art Therapy   94
11 The Talking Cures   100
12 Meditation   109
13 Spiritual Healing   116
14 The Way Forward   120

Glossary   131
Useful Addresses   134
Bibliography   143
Index   145

Introduction

When I was diagnosed with cancer five years ago, I chose to seek whatever help was available to me, both from the orthodox medical establishment and from other sources. The Bristol Cancer Help Centre quickly became one of the most powerful factors in my cancer journey. It supported me as a *whole* person: body, mind and spirit. Without the support of the Centre I would have found it difficult to know what direction to take, how to focus my mind, or pull together so quickly all the available possibilities. After a cancer diagnosis, there is an overwhelming urgency to know as much as possible about what is happening to you on all levels. Quite simply, when you are faced with a life-threatening disease it suddenly dawns on you that *this is it*. The future is *now*. You can't put off living anymore.

Even five years ago it was difficult to find holistic therapies on offer within the NHS. Those who sought them, like the Centre's founder Penny Brohn, had to do so independently, normally without the blessing of the orthodox medical world. Although this situation is beginning to change, Bristol-type centres are still specialists in their field, as are those in the orthodox world. It makes sense to seek both options.

For newly diagnosed cancer patients who face all the associated anxieties, stresses and confusion, the Centre's approach can be invaluable. For those who have been diagnosed with secondaries and initially put all their trust in orthodox treatment, the discovery that cancer has returned can be devasting. At this time, a new, self-motivated approach on a deeper level can be re-energising: a powerful tool to use alongside your conventional treatment.

Whatever your circumstances, I suggest you dip into this book and find what appeals to *you*. The essence of the holistic approach is that it is *self-motivated* and self-responsible – not driven from without: it is very personal to each individual, and taking the whole Bristol programme as a package may not be appropriate. So choose, and learn to follow what feels right for you. This can be a self-empowering process.

Much has been written about the Bristol Cancer Help Centre's work, both good and bad. *The Bristol Experience* seeks to place the Centre in a social and historical context, clear away the myths and outline its work in layman's terms. The first section concentrates mostly on the Centre's history (including a frank and full account of the Chilvers episode which caused such a stir in 1990), and the second section is about its present-day work and hopes for the future.

Places like the Bristol Cancer Help Centre really can help guide you on your journey. As I have discovered, it is a journey which does not end with the "cure" or remission of cancer, but which becomes a way of life and self-responsibility, enhancing not only the lives of those with cancer, but of all those around them. Cancer *can* be a beginning – not an end.

Jane Metcalfe

PART ONE

1

The Bristol Experience

Liz Hodgkinson's account

The twelve people sitting in a circle looked, at first sight, normal and healthy enough. They were talking, laughing and smiling and seemed a little nervous as one often is in strange surroundings and when meeting new people. There was a slight atmosphere of the protective cover of suspicion, of keeping our own space.

There were nine women and three men, all but me either cancer patients or relatives of cancer patients. We were meeting in the relaxation room of the Bristol Cancer Help Centre, which has seen thousands of cancer patients since it first opened in 1980.

The relaxation room was furnished with what looked like outdoor or garden chairs, made of plastic and with flowery foam cushions. You might expect to find them in the garden department of a John Lewis store, but when you tilted the armrest, they reclined. They were relaxation chairs, and extremely comfortable. The room was very large and had some peculiar-looking musical instruments and a mini-piano in one corner. A large board for slides and other visual aids was also there, indicating that this was a teaching and seminar room as well as a place to relax. A brand-new pale blue fitted carpet was on the floor.

It was a Monday morning, about half past twelve, and most of us had arrived that morning. Two of the men – one a shy boy of sixteen – were there as "supporters", for members of their family who had been diagnosed with cancer.

We were a motley crowd indeed, united only by the cancer diagnosis. I was there "for real", as a cancer patient, even though I wasn't, and my task was to try to make an imaginative leap into understanding what it must be like to know you are living with cancer. All but one of the women had breast cancer – the commonest kind of cancer which brings patients to Bristol. The other woman patient had a malignant melanoma. The one male cancer patient had lung cancer: he had been a lifelong smoker who was able to kick the habit instantly once the diagnosis had been made. He had been the proprietor of a newsagent's business, and was accompanied by his son, a TV executive in his thirties. There were two housewives in their sixties: one was upper-crust with a prosperous husband and apparently enviably comfortable lifestyle, while the other was working-class. She was with her grandson, the shy and appealing sixteen-year-old boy.

Another of the patients was a single woman in her forties. A lay preacher who worked in a city library, she had an engaging throwaway wit. There was a retired music teacher in her seventies, a woman who had started up her own Welsh-speaking school, a publishing company and who also made her own shoes, she said, to the great amusement of us all.

One woman was a doctor. In her thirties, she had two small children. Another woman in her thirties was a single parent with a nine-year-old son. Currently living on state benefits, she was a mature student and an active member of her local Labour party.

There were two nurses: one was in her early thirties, the other was in her fifties, married with grown-up children whose husband was about to be made redundant.

They had come from these various walks of life to sample the holistic care at Bristol, and to try, by whatever means, to reduce the fear and stress which had gripped them ever since the diagnosis of cancer had been made, and cast a grim shadow over their lives. They were not looking for a miracle cure – Bristol has never claimed or offered this – but to try to gain a positive outlook and also, if possible, to strengthen their immune systems so that further cancers would not be able to take hold. Already, with several patients, the cancer had spread to other sites in their bodies. Several of the breast cancer patients had already had mastectomies; most had undergone chemotherapy and radiotherapy. Most were relatively new cancer patients and all wondered what the week would hold.

As we met and got to know each other a little better over the vegan lunch, it became apparent that by no means were their doctors unequivocally in favour of the Bristol approach. Some doctors had taken the attitude that going to Bristol could probably do no harm – although a damning report published a few years earlier had alleged that going to Bristol *could* do cancer patients harm, and the Centre was only now beginning to recover from this almost fatal blow – but few members of the orthodox medical profession believed it could do any lasting good, at least compared with their laboratory-tested treatments.

We were all here to experience a completely different approach to cancer from the orthodox, an approach which didn't rely on high-tech drugs, genetic manipulation or radiation, but which worked to strengthen the mind, body and spirit – and particularly the spirit – through nutrition, relaxation, counselling, spiritual healing, massage, art therapy and music therapy, plus group and individual sessions.

It was the so-called "gentle approach", for which the Bristol Centre – through a series of television programmes, many books and much high-profile coverage, including being opened in its current premises by Prince Charles in 1983 – had become world-famous.

Since the Centre started in a modest way in 1980, it had become a nerve centre for all that was new and avant-garde in complementary approaches to the most feared disease of all time. The emphasis had always been on complementary rather than alternative approaches, therapies which enhance and support orthodox medicine rather than attempting to supplant it.

Never had Bristol promised to cure cancer, which is why it has always been called a "help" centre. Most of the people who were gathered at this residents' week, as well as those who had gone there in the past, had been patients in the orthodox system as well. In the early days, most had sought out Bristol only when they reached the stage of desperation, when they had been told that there was no more the doctors could do for them. Some at this point had made miraculous recoveries, while others, terminally ill, had died. But now, as the people on this particular week showed, patients were starting to come soon after diagnosis, to optimise their chances and to try to give themselves the best quality of life possible, with or without cancer.

Our main therapist for the week was Barbara Siddall, a pleasant-faced, white-haired lady with a decided penchant for hippyish clothes and co-ordinating pastel colours. She had a beautiful voice, which is a great asset for a therapist, and a distinctly calming presence.

There was also a qualified doctor present, Jo Shawcross, who was tall and slim and favoured Liberty print skirts and scarves. From the first, Bristol had always insisted that there should be a qualified orthodox doctor present at the sessions. Jo was still working in the NHS but over the years she had become convinced, as are an increasing number of doctors, that, when confronted with an emotive disease such as cancer, most patients need more than cold-hearted surgery, chemotherapy and radiotherapy, however successful these treatments might be in themselves to reduce or obliterate the tumour.

Cancer remains, for everybody, the big fear. AIDS cannot come anywhere near it as, for most of us, this disease remains relatively remote. How many of us know an AIDS sufferer? Yet all of us are, or have been, intimately acquainted with a cancer patient. There is little in life to compare with the knowledge that you have cells in your body which have gone out of control and are attacking you. When your body starts to attack itself, this is often the time to rethink priorities and attitudes, as there is not a simple pill or operation which can, without fail, guarantee to cure such a complex and capricious disease as cancer.

My own purpose during this week was to try to close the gap between being a cancer patient and not being a cancer patient. I realise that those who have never been confronted with such a diagnosis can hardly begin to imagine what it must be like. The patients said that even their cancer specialists didn't know – as they had never actually had to cope with a diagnosis themselves. We were all here mainly to discuss and find effective ways of dealing with the emotional impact of cancer.

At first none of us knew each other. But although we were all very different, and came from a huge variety of social and educational backgrounds, the group bonded in emotion from the start. I realised that few of the patients knew much about the holistic approach, in spite of a plethora of books and articles on holistic medicine appearing over the previous decade.

The holistic approach is still little understood and remains a minority pursuit, I discovered. It also became clear that when the chips are down, most people would like to be able to rely on orthodox medicine, which seems so reassuring with its scans, checks, white coats, qualified personnel and hierarchical set-up. The fact that, with the majority of cancers, little significant progress has been made towards a one hundred per cent cure over the past sixty years has not lessened most people's faith, and all of the patients present at Bristol had experienced the full gamut of orthodox treatment.

But the fact that orthodox medicine cannot guarantee to cure cancer does not mean that nothing can be done. It doesn't mean that we can't enjoy life for however long we've got left – and of course, nobody knows this for sure, whether or not they have cancer. It's just that a cancer diagnosis confronts people, often for the very first time, with their own mortality. It's at this time that people may come to appreciate that they are temporary, that they are not going to go on for ever.

For the first time, these people at Bristol had been confronted with the possibility of death and they realised: I don't want to die, not just yet. I want to be with my family, continue my career, my life, for a good few years yet. I'm not ready to go, not yet!

But back to the lunch table – and the famous, or notorious, Bristol Diet. From the first, Bristol has been known for its natural, vegetarian diet and on this week, as on every residents' week, the diet excited much comment. For most of the patients, who may need this gentle diet more than those who are in good health, it seemed decidedly peculiar. Throughout the week, the diet was to arouse more comment, hostility and discussion than any other single aspect of the Bristol therapy.

The first Bristol Diet book was published in the early eighties, and was written by the first doctor in residence there, Dr Alec Forbes, a former consultant physician. Before he took up his voluntary post at Bristol, he had travelled round the world to try to discover which were the healthiest diets. He had come up with this low-fat, high-fibre, high-raw, low dairy produce, meat-free, organic approach to nutrition which has formed the basis of the Bristol menus ever since.

At the time, the Bristol Diet, as it came to be known, was considered decidedly cranky, but over the years it has been modified so that it no longer represents quite such a shock to most people's systems. Even so, the patients on this week regarded it with something approaching suspicion, and I cannot claim they became overly enthusiastic as the week progressed. Even from the very first meal we had together, on this Monday lunchtime, several spoke with nostalgia of the "real" food they'd enjoyed at the Little Chef or Happy Eater on the way to the Centre.

On that first day we had shepherdess pie (shepherd's pie without the meat or the salt – or the taste, as some commented), mixed salad with dressing, and fruit crumble. We all missed a cup of real coffee after lunch – and this definitely wasn't on the menu. Only ersatz versions such as Barleycup or Bambu were available, and though looking rather like instant coffee, didn't live up to expectations. Nor did they give the caffeine lift that so many of us have come to expect from our post-prandial beverage. But we had to wean ourselves off this while at Bristol. Coffee is not available at the Centre. If we didn't fancy the coffee substitutes, we could have herb tea. Or, if we really had to, a cup of real tea, with soya milk. Drinking cows' milk is definitely not encouraged, although there was a small jug of it there for the hardliners.

At first, everybody was desperately trying to keep their spirits up by laughing and joking, but after lunch, and as the day wore on, several people became rather weepy. Cancer constitutes a severe emotional crisis whenever it is diagnosed. Nobody expects to get it – but nobody can be guaranteed immune, however apparently healthy the life that may have been led.

In the afternoon of the first day, after many postmortems on the lunch, we reassembled in the relaxation room for an introductory talk on holistic principles. Barbara Siddall conducted the meeting. Her initial message was that if ever you take away hope, you destroy the will to live. Some people though, she added, had found to their surprise that cancer was the best thing that ever happened to them, as it gave them a chance to set the reset button of their lives and re-evaluate their priorities and relationships. Out of every crisis, she said, came an opportunity – an observation which has now become something of a cliché, but which more or less encapsulates the philosophy of Bristol.

The group were asked to share their experiences and emotions following their cancer diagnosis. Many were easily moved to tears in the safe setting of the group, and talked quite easily – or "shared" in holistic centre parlance – their feelings when told they had cancer. The overwhelming reaction was one of fear. Another was of isolation: suddenly, they felt alone. A very common further reaction was that of ignorance, as they suddenly realised they knew very little about cancer, and what they could expect in the way of treatment.

For all, it was a severe shock to the system and to their lives. Few had been able to talk openly about their cancer to their families, and this had also come as something of a shock. In several cases, their nearest and dearest weren't very near and dear at all – in fact, they felt let down and resentful. Some relatives panicked, others simply did not want to hear about it or discuss it. Some family members, we heard, took the attitude that the cancer might go away if you didn't admit it was there. Several said that their friends had ignored them since learning of the cancer. One patient said that her sister had not spoken to her since the diagnosis.

Fear grips not only the cancer patient, but all those in the family. Husbands, wives or partners came out particularly badly. Instead of being supportive, as one might have imagined, they made the whole thing worse by being unable to confront it or discuss it. This frequently had the effect of making the cancer patient feel responsible for other people's stress, thus adding to his or her own.

The afternoon discussion served as a potent reminder of how greatly we still fear cancer, even though in many ways it has now come out into the open. We no longer feel we have to speak of cancer in hushed or whispered tones, but although we can now all say the word, this has done little to diminish the fear that continues to surround the disease.

When faced with a cancer diagnosis, even the most confident, seemingly successful and assertive person can feel weak and helpless, vulnerable, a victim. You realise that after all you are weak and frail, and that however rich and powerful you might be, not all the money, position or public acclaim in the world can prevent these cancer cells from proliferating inside your body. Nor can you by an act of will stop them from spreading and attacking healthy organs. Although certain lifestyles and attitudes may reduce the risk – theoretically – there is nothing you can do to guarantee absolutely that you will never get cancer.

So, said Barbara, with her many years' experience of running weeks like this, the main point overall is to try to stop feeling like a helpless victim and put yourself back in charge. This, she reminded us, was not so easy, as it is hard work empowering yourself when you are constantly reminded of how weak your body might be. But, putting yourself back in charge and inculcating a positive attitude could, she said, affect the cancer cells, which are basically weak and unordered and chaotic. The whole idea of the residents' week was to learn strategies which can help to strengthen the body's self-healing systems so that it can more effectively deal with the cancer cells, zapping them and depriving them of their power.

On this introductory afternoon, Barbara went round members of the group asking what, if any, complementary therapies they had tried, or which had been offered at their hospitals. One or two said they had been offered cancer counselling, and some had been offered spiritual healing. One patient said that through her cancer, she had come to discover a healing ability in herself.

Mostly, though, we learned, anything "alternative" or natural had been self-sought rather than being offered in the hospital setting. One patient said she had to fight the breast surgeon who told her that complementary therapies were not necessary, as he and his team could do all that was required.

A cry of "arrogance" went up from the group. Barbara reminded us that many members of the medical profession can appear to be arrogant and do not want others threatening their methods with unorthodox therapies. None of this would matter if doctors had a guaranteed cure for cancer. But as yet, they haven't.

It soon became obvious that even this group of people, who were more open-minded than the majority as regards medical treatment – otherwise they wouldn't have booked themselves in at Bristol – did not know much about complementary therapies. Several had read every book they could get hold of on cancer, yet understandably were still confused as to what had caused their cancer.

Barbara's talk, which was wide-ranging, went on to discuss the role of vitamin and mineral supplements. These are, and always have been, very much recommended at Bristol, but are still largely derided by orthodox specialists. Most cancer specialists – oncologists – take the attitude that so long as we eat a good, varied diet, there is no need for expensive supplements. Yet there is increasing evidence from studies that vitamin supplements can powerfully boost the immune system and other healing systems in the body, particularly with people whose systems have been compromised by drug treatment or radiation, or by a devastating disease.

Dairy produce is not recommended at Bristol as it is considered demanding to the system. Also, it contains a lot of artificial hormones. As we now know, many forms of breast cancer are hormone-dependent. Most of the nutritional experts attached to Bristol take the attitude that we simply don't need dairy produce after we are weaned, any more than adult animals need milk. It is a food only for infants, we were reminded.

Barbara then went on to talk about the importance of breathing properly, and this constitutes a large part of her therapy. Where your breath is, that's where your thoughts will be, she told us. It is common when in a state of stress or panic to breathe shallowly, and this has the effect of increasing the panic and stress. Deep breathing can bring about altered, or heightened consciousness, if practised enough, and with it a calm, positive attitude.

She reminded us that nowadays many of us live in our heads, through the intellect. But in order to become properly well, we must be able to still the mind and concentrate on the emotions and gut reactions.

The point is that however intellectual or rational or logical we might consider ourselves to be, when confronted with a cancer diagnosis, it is feelings that overwhelm. There may be feelings of anger, of resignation, of guilt, fear, terror, hopelessness. But whatever they are, they are always feelings and emotions. Mainly, at first, the feelings will be negative, as the commonest reaction when faced with a cancer diagnosis is: why me? Why have I been given this death sentence? Why is my body attacking itself?

One time-honoured way to combat negative feelings, we were advised, is to allow proper time for rest and relaxation. We would be learning this during our week at Bristol. We had to learn to allow all thoughts, whether negative or not, to come to the surface and not be kept down all the time. The energy involved in trying to keep unwelcome thoughts at the back of our mind, firmly repressed, constitutes an extra strain on the system.

Most people, said Barbara, whether in good health or not, do not allow enough time for rest and relaxation. While at Bristol, at least, time would be set aside for both group and individual relaxation, rest and meditation.

The word "meditation" still has the power to conjure up chanting yogis, ageing hippies, navel-gazing. For many, the very word presents a negative image. This, said Barbara, is because we fear looking deep into ourselves.

We then moved on to discuss a highly contentious and hotly debated issue – whether there is such a thing as the "cancer personality". It is a debate which has been raging for literally thousands of years, and is still not resolved. The present-day interpretation is that there are so many different kinds of cancer, and it affects so very many people, that if there is such a thing as the cancer personality, then we must all have it. In our group were single women, divorced, married and widowed women. Some had high-flying careers, some were housewives, some were retired or unwaged. Some were parents, some were not. Some had a deep religious faith, others had none. Some were strident or assertive, others were timid or passive. Some seemed to have a strong purpose in life, while others were drifting. There was no one outstanding personality characteristic which you could point to and say: oh yes, now I understand it. This is the cancer personality, as exemplified by all those present. All that this particular group had in common was that we were white, heterosexual and roughly middle-class. But cancer itself is no respecter of race, class or sexual orientation.

The BCHC is highly enthusiastic about American psychologist Lawrence LeShan's idea of singing your own song, finding your own voice and expressing yourself, rather than simply and unthinkingly treading in paths laid down by other people. It is the frustration which comes from not singing your own song which predisposes to cancer by causing stress and depressing the immune system, according to Le Shan. But sometimes, said Barbara, there can be a potent block about finding your own song. Perhaps we fear rejection from the outside world, perhaps we fear we may not be very good after all at what we secretly long to do. The trouble with a cancer diagnosis is that it can freeze everything, cutting us off from ourselves even more. It is basically the ability to "find ourselves" that the Bristol experience hopes to set in motion.

Some people may believe that they "themselves" may not be very nice, so they try to be somebody else, a nicer person than the "real" them. When people think this, they try to meet others' needs rather than their own, and try to discount their own personal goals. It is this continual suppression of personal needs which may possibly predispose to cancer, according to theories largely accepted by Bristol.

The Centre also believes wholeheartedly in the value of counselling. A counsellor can help patients to recognise repeating and unhelpful patterns, to remind us that we have choices and that we are powerful, if we choose to be. An illness such as cancer, which is such a very serious crisis, can make us aware of choices we previously never knew we had, choices which can either help to heal us, or perhaps make us worse. Talking about attitudes to cancer is particularly important, as few diseases are so isolating, and the majority of people still find cancer difficult to discuss.

The emphasis at Bristol, right from the start, has been on spiritual rather than physical healing. We were reminded that the Centre itself grew out of the healing ministry of Canon Christopher Pilkington, a rector in the town during the seventies, and co-founder of the Bristol Centre.

The group members were asked to describe their experiences of cancer. Different reactions emerged: there was the shock, of course, but also for some even a feeling of relief, of knowing the enemy at last. There was great fear, fear of the unknown, and also worry about family members. And yet, as with most things, the diagnosis of cancer, even at this initial stage of self-realisation, was not seen to be entirely bad. Several people spoke of the unexpected kindness of friends, family and work colleagues, kindnesses they had not known were there.

The last bit of the first afternoon had us dividing into small groups to discuss again, but this time more intimately, individual experiences of cancer. One resident, the sole male cancer patient present, said he was worried about his wife and how she could cope if he suddenly went. Another resident said she didn't want an operation as her husband had had cancer, and all the operations going – yet they didn't save him. Insomnia was a very common problem, caused possibly by submerged worries surfacing at night, and in some cases caused by the medication.

After our discussion, we then reconvened in the big group to share our experiences. One assertive resident said it was a good idea to take a tape recorder when seeing the doctor, and placing it firmly on his or her desk when a consultation was taking place. That made doctors very careful of what they were saying, she informed us. Everybody laughed with recognition at this. She added that the presence of the tape recorder meant that they took you more seriously, and were less patronising than they might otherwise have been. The first afternoon session thus ended. It had been surprisingly hard work and emotionally draining. We rested in our rooms, had a walk, took a bath, chatted – whatever – until it was time for supper.

On the first evening, after supper, we met in the sitting room which abounded with furry toys left or donated by previous residents. At first they seemed naff to me, but then I picked one up and found it surprisingly comforting. Most of the other residents picked up a toy – they seemed irresistible, and offered us a chance to regress a little. There was to be an entertainment programme in the evening, of songs and stories by a very thin couple called John and Fay. Both had been very ill with chronic fatigue syndrome, and singing and performing was part of their therapy on the way to recovery. So, at Bristol, we can all learn to help each other.

One thing immediately apparent at Bristol is that there are plenty of helpers. You as a resident don't have to do a thing, and this aspect was highly appreciated. There were heartfelt comments about how nice it was not to have to cook – even if the vegan fare was not universally appreciated – and how pleasant it was to come away to be cosseted.

Yet, during that first evening, and although most had left home only hours before, they queued up to use the telephone to contact their families. Cancer patients, I realised, often feel guilty for being ill and inflicting this burden on others, guilty for taking time off, for spending money on themselves, guilty for not coping, guilty that their systems have broken down and guilty for upsetting everybody and causing trouble.

The day had been tiring and several people dropped off during John and Fay's concert, which in itself was something to come to terms with, consisting as it did of Tibetan overtone chanting. "What's that strange noise?" asked one resident as John attempted to sing several vowel sounds at once. This form of Tibetan chanting with its distinct New Age connotations, is supposed to be a form of heightening consciousness.

It is very noticeable right from the start that Bristol is mainly run by women. Two women – Pat Pilkington and Penny Brohn – were responsible for starting the Centre and, currently, most of its doctors, helpers and therapists are women. There are about fifty staff altogether, including part-timers. The overwhelming presence of women was a salutary reminder that in holistic health care, they remain in the vanguard. Around two-thirds of the patients who attend Bristol are women, and two-thirds of these are breast cancer patients. Because of the large number of helpers, we kept seeing people we had not come across before. Some residents found this rather disconcerting, as very often, when we were discussing or "sharing", a new person would come in and join the circle.

Every morning started off in the same way, with a half-hour stretch-and-breathe session (optional) before breakfast at half past eight. Not everybody made those "early morning" sessions, although all agreed in principle that they were an excellent way to start the day, and the exercises themselves were extremely gentle, suitable for seriously ill people as well as those in good health.

The breakfast aroused as much suspicion and comment as the other meals. Used to bacon and eggs, or at least, to toast, butter and marmalade, people looked askance at the "rice porridge" – rice pudding made without salt or sugar. Yet it was flavoured with something, and had the comforting feel of an invalid food. It also had skin on it – the tastiest bit, as ever. There was homemade wholemeal bread every morning, with soya margarine and unsweetened jam, and fresh fruit was always available. The muesli, soaked overnight in soya milk, had some takers, but the most popular breakfast item was toast. There was a six-slice toaster in continual use.

From the first, it became apparent how near the surface deep and conflicting emotions were. People who probably wouldn't allow themselves to show emotion in their ordinary lives became very weepy. Emotions welled up and were discussed, or shared. In this group, nobody felt isolated but all felt supported and safe. In a way, this was a potent tribute to Bristol because all were able to be emotional. Most of the residents said they were unable to show much emotion in their everyday lives, partly because they were unused to it, and partly because they were nervous of upsetting those around them.

We kept being reminded that we were not responsible for other people's emotions, but most of us have been given messages all our lives that we are. There was a lot of unlearning to do on that week and unlearning, like learning, is never easy – especially when certain attitudes have become ingrained, a long-term habit.

Throughout the week, residents were encouraged to put their experiences into words – not always the simplest task. But something which came out loud and clear from the start was that once you have a diagnosis of cancer, you feel very separate from other people, no longer connected. Attractive to everybody in our group was that here, at least, a majority of the people had cancer, so knew what it was like. Treatments and reactions to treatments were endlessly swapped over meals and free time during the week.

Why was everybody here? That was the question asked at the start of the week, and at times throughout the programme. It seemed that this was an easy one to answer: they were looking for help, for the kind of help they had been unable to obtain in any other way. They were looking for coping mechanisms, strategies that would help them reduce their fear and, if they couldn't beat the cancer, at least they could learn to live with it.

They wanted to discover ways of coping with stress which didn't do harm, such as smoking, drinking, indulging in addictive sex or binge eating. Two of the patients smoked and had to keep going out for their fags. The one resident living on state benefit admitted that, out of an income of £90 a week, she spent £30 on cigarettes; smoking, for the time being, helped to reduce the stress.

Barbara Siddall reminded us throughout the week that we were, above all, here to learn to love ourselves, and not to be too hard on ourselves. In fact, being hard on oneself, overly critical, emerged time and again in discussions as a serious problem. Members of the group had got into the habit of being hard on themselves at every opportunity, of blaming themselves for the cancer, for not being good at things, for not earning enough money, not being good daughters, wives, husbands or parents, or whatever.

Most were still very much in shock over their cancers, as all had been relatively recently diagnosed. One had not been expected to live until the end of the year, yet here she was, apparently fit and well. She said, though, that her breast cancer had spread to her liver – a prime place for secondaries and an organ which, unlike a breast, you can't just cut out.

During this week, all residents and their supporters had individual sessions. There were consultations with the doctor, where treatments, medication and side-effects were discussed. Every evening, a night nurse came in, in case any of the residents became ill during the night. Several did, although whether this was owing to the cancer, to the medication, or the "healing crisis" which often happens when people are confronted with their own deep emotions, was not always apparent. Probably a mixture of all three.

The diet may have had something to answer for, because several residents developed stomach upsets. A radical change of diet is always liable to affect the bowels, and the idea that a sudden change of diet makes you suddenly wonderfully healthy is simply not true. Both the body and the mind have to have time to adjust. All the extra fibre may have been difficult for some to handle, as well.

Undoubtedly the talk that attracted most interest was that given by nutritionist Ute Brookman, who has been associated with the Centre ever since its inception. Much, it seemed, was bad for you, with dairy products and meat at the top of the list. Cancer patients, Ute said, had to be particularly careful about their diet, as their treatments were often extremely toxic, and they had to be sure not to add to the toxic load.

"What do I do if I have a friend round for a cup of tea?" asked one resident. She was worried about having to offer soya milk or tea substitutes, and for this not being taken as proper hospitality. Others felt they could not possibly condemn, as they saw it, their families to the Bristol diet, even though this is a lot less strict than in the early days.

Only a minority of patients stick rigidly to the diet once they go home, we were told. Most take bits and pieces, and Ute admitted that changing your diet radically can add to stress in the short term. Many residents were highly defensive about their ordinary diets, and there was great resistance to change. Diet always provokes heated discussion and one or two residents felt insulted that every food item they mentioned seemed to be on the forbidden list. But the message came out loud and clear: eat lots of vegetables and fruit, avoid dairy produce where possible, cut down or avoid altogether meat and meat products, and increase your fibre intake.

Caffeine in all its forms is bad, and alcohol is best avoided if you've got cancer, especially if yours has spread to the liver. Organic produce was highly recommended and, for preference, is always used at the Centre. Some residents complained that there was no way they could afford to buy organic, although organic vegetables and fruit are far cheaper than meat or fish.

The point about the diet is that it's one thing you can control, if you want to. You alone can decide what you want to eat. What nobody wanted to convey was that, if you didn't stick rigidly to the diet, your cancer would instantly get worse and your lifespan be decreased. The point is that by eating the healthiest diet possible you are maximising internal conditions so that healing can take place. You are making it easier for the cancer to eradicate itself from your system. The other point made during Ute's evening talk was that changing your diet gives instant empowerment. If you go to a shop and buy a pound of organic carrots, you have achieved something towards your own self-healing. You have made an important start, an essential first step on the day. Our diet is one of the few things we can change about our lives: other things may not be so easy, or even possible.

On another evening, we were given a talk by Pat Pilkington, the Centre's co-founder. Pat must have given this talk many times before, but it came out fresh and new. She is a slim, elegant, well-dressed and warm-hearted woman, the wife of Canon Christopher Pilkington, and her talk was highly popular. She told us how the present imposing premises had grown out of the healing centre set up by herself and her husband in Bristol, and by Penny Brohn, who worked at the healing ministry as an acupuncturist before becoming a cancer patient herself.

Healing, said Pat, seemed to be the most powerful thing that could be offered as it involved no organised religion, no medication, no visits to the doctor and no argument. It was accomplished by the simple laying on of hands, and yet miracles frequently resulted. Pat explained healing by saying that it was like a radio wave, and there was an answering response.

In its early days, Bristol attracted so much publicity that it became world-famous, Pat said, and the six-part TV series which was broadcast in 1983 was the first time that a complementary healing centre had been taken at all seriously in the UK. But, Pat hinted darkly, it was that series of six programmes, which initially seemed to be so positive and which had given complementary therapies such a boost, which was ultimately to prove their undoing – the outcome of which was that the Centre almost went bankrupt and almost had to close.

But the TV series and subsequent books written by Bristol people – therapists, doctors and patients – throughout the eighties, helped to get holistic and complementary therapies incorporated into a number of NHS hospitals, and the message spread. At the same time, Bristol doctors and workers were asked to speak at international conferences around the world. Bristol people appeared on television programmes worldwide, and a number of Bristol-like centres were set up in other countries, often staffed by former Bristol people.

As Pat spoke, we were reminded that, since its earliest days, a kind of glamour has surrounded the Bristol Centre, a glamour which still clings round it, in spite of all its vicissitudes in the early nineties, and the fact that few of the original charismatic people who put Bristol on the international map are still working at the Centre.

By now it was the middle of the week, and the days – early morning exercises, group discussions, individual sessions, had fallen into a pattern. Although we all had been complete strangers at the beginning of the week, the group had by now become a cohesive force and members had genuine concern for and empathy with each other. We discussed such problems as not being able to go out to work when you've got cancer and having demanding treatments such as chemotherapy, and the difficulty of managing on disability payments and benefits. What is not always realised is that cancer can make you extremely poor: several patients had had to give up their jobs, or take extended sick leave. One decided to move house after the diagnosis. The lack of money and feeling too ill for work adds, of course, to the already considerable stress.

Group discussions included sharing information about which benefits were available, and how you could get a home help and other kinds of care. Several of the residents realised just how ignorant they were about the social services, income support and so on. Sharing of actual hard information was an extremely valuable part of the week.

Anybody who has had cancer will know that very often the treatment makes you feel worse than the disease, and that there can be very bad side-effects from chemotherapy. Loss of hair is a well-known one, but there can be others, such as mouth ulcers, sickness and a general feeling of debilitation which can take days, sometimes weeks, to get over. One or two women said they preferred to undergo a mastectomy rather than the medical treatment, but if secondaries develop, they may have to have it as well as the mutilating surgery. One thing that emerged very clearly is that there are no easy answers to cancer. It is the very unpredictability of the disease, of not knowing whether you have finally "beaten" it which causes the greatest fear.

As the week went by, the relaxation and meditation sessions – new to most of the residents – became more popular. It became evident that all the patients were under the most enormous stress, stress that possibly they had not previously allowed themselves to express or acknowledge. But in this group setting, they were able to voice precisely how they felt. The message that was repeated time and again – and it can't be repeated too often, to cancer patients especially – was that we must be kind to ourselves, and not judge ourselves too harshly. We must do whatever we can to make our minds happy, as this will have a beneficial effect on the body.

Healing sessions are all individual, and these took place in the chapel. One of the aspects which decided the Pilkingtons and the Brohns to buy the convent as a cancer centre was that it already had a chapel. Several residents were initially suspicious of the spiritual healing, as they had been of the diet, and yet this was enormously appreciated. I would say that of any single aspect, the spiritual healing was the most popular, and had the most dramatic effects.

Nobody, not even the most sceptical, remained unmoved by the spiritual healing, which on one or two people had a startling physical effect. Perhaps the general spiritual atmosphere of the Bristol Centre, by which I mean calm, harmonious and gentle, rather than embracing any particular religious dogma – made the patients more receptive to spiritual healing than they might have been in another context. The fact that the week was residential helped the atmosphere to become more concentrated, and this possibly helped the healing to be more effective.

The kindness and positive attitude of the healers, therapists and helpers were enormously appreciated. All the staff at Bristol take a lot of care with their appearance, and this can have a subtle healing effect. It says: I care enough about my appearance and its effect on others to take trouble. Also, the different outfits worn by Bristol staff emphasised the individuality of the place, the fact that our uniqueness is respected.

Art therapy is an important aspect of the Bristol experience. This, now becoming increasingly popular in complementary care, is different from painting, or trying to paint, pretty or obviously meaningful pictures. But here again, there was the most enormous lack of confidence and complaints of: I can't paint, I can't draw, I've got no sense of colour, I haven't picked up a paintbrush since I was at school. We were all asked to visualise the same thing – ourselves as we were, or would like to be, and after a few stares at the blank sheet, we all managed to get going. Barbara Siddall reminded us that we were not there to draw a convincing self-portrait or a likeness, but to do an image of ourselves, our health, our relationships, our view of what we wanted for ourselves.

The results could not have been more different. Some people drew or painted hearts and flowers, others painted blocks of colour. Some used pastels to gain a muted effect, while others used bright primary colours. One patient drew a complicated molecular structure. One or two preferred to work with clay. After a rather nervous start, we all enjoyed the art therapy, and most of us made up our minds to buy paint, brushes and paper and keep it up when we got home. Art therapy was immediately therapeutic, and most of us became completely absorbed in the images we were creating.

It was quite surprising, perhaps, that in view of the initial protestations, a considerable amount of unrecognised artistic ability emerged. The very fact that the residents were able to make marks on paper which looked aesthetically pleasing and which actually meant something, vastly increased self-confidence.

One aspect of the Bristol week which was particularly pleasing was that great care was taken of the carers. On all residents' weeks, supporters are encouraged to come and join in the programmes, at a reduced rate. Supporters attend the group discussions and also have individual sessions and supporters' meetings. On our week, there were just two supporters – the sixteen-year-old boy who was supporting his grandmother, and the son with his father. I think the supporters got as much out of the week – for themselves – as did the patients.

Music therapy was also an important part of the Bristol programme. Here, we were asked not so much to make tunes as to express ourselves in sound. Again, the hurdles of self-consciousness and embarrassment had to be overcome. There was a strange collection of instruments – most of which did not require any great expertise at least to make a satisfyingly loud sound, and they were mainly of the percussion variety – glockenspiel, drums, tambourines, maracas, Chinese temple bells, cymbals. The noise we all made together maybe wasn't very harmonious, but it was fun, brought the group even closer together and enabled us to shed yet more inhibitions.

By the fourth day, many of us were feeling tired. I, who was in good health and not a cancer patient, surprised myself by nodding off in some of the group sessions, and not waking up in the mornings until half past seven. Normally, I consider I've done well if I sleep until six. For many of the patients, going to bed represented another form of stress as it had been many years since they had enjoyed a good night's sleep. This meant, of course, that they too were liable to nod off during the day.

Barbara said that she had noticed during her many years of running residents' weeks, that a lot of cumulative tiredness came out, as a kind of reaction to all the new stuff which was being imparted and assimilated. Most of us, she said, don't allow ourselves enough rest but imagine we must keep going whatever, and not let the side or ourselves down. Also, few of us are any good at putting ourselves first. Sometimes, a diagnosis of cancer enabled us to do this, and remember that we must look after ourselves first if we are to be strong enough to be effective.

Also, said Barbara, many of us are not very good at living in the present moment. We live either in the past or in the future. One of the most insidious aspects of fear is of course fear of the future, of what might happen. This presents itself even more vividly with cancer patients, who worry that they may not even have a future, than with others. Much of the fear which accompanies cancer is that which comes from projecting ourselves into the future: what if we can't look after our families? What if we don't live to see our children grow up? What if our tumour spreads? What if we develop secondaries?

None of these fears will stop any of these things from happening: on the contrary, fearing things may well bring them about. But once we can start to live in the present moment, our fears decrease. At least, we can enjoy today. It says of course in the Bible that we should have no thought for the morrow, and this is something cancer patients must learn to imbibe.

Thursday afternoon was Andy's day. Andy is a masseur, and he has been coming to the Bristol Centre for very many years. Several of the patients were nervous of the massage, partly because they had bits missing and felt mutilated and ashamed, and partly because Andy was a man. However, those who had the massage – the loving touch – were very pleased they had agreed to it.

Andy runs a massage school in the town, and uses essential oils to ease out accumulated tension and stress. He managed to massage a lot of stress out of my shoulders and neck, which is where it gathers for most people, and the massage was a highly enjoyable and relaxing experience. On other days, shiatsu massage is available, and some patients prefer this, as it is done through clothes.

Andy said that a lot of cancer patients are very nervous about exhibiting their bodies, especially if they have had extensive surgery. Also, many are not used to being touched, except sexually or by members of their families. Touch works from the outside in, as other therapies are designed to work from the inside out. We need both – and Bristol provides both.

At the residents' weeks, nobody has to do anything which feels wrong, which they don't quite like, or which bothers them. The programme is very full, and quite demanding, but if you want to spend all day in bed, that's up to you. Some of the patients did have a day in bed, not feeling up to joining the group on some occasions.

On Thursday evening, there was a party and get-together with circle dancing. The party included wine, peanuts and Cadbury's Flakes, which were a great treat as several patients had felt genuinely deprived of their chocolate ration!

The circle dancing was surprisingly exhausting, but we all enjoyed it, as, once again, it brought the group together in a non-threatening, non-competitive way. Again, there were initial cries of: I can't dance, don't ask me – but of course, everybody can do circle dancing, as we soon discovered. The evening ended with our retired music teacher from Wales entertaining us all with songs, hymns, classical and pop music. Although initially reluctant to play for us, Lily quickly blossomed into an entertainer, and seemed able to play any song, any tune, that was requested. And in the end, even those who insisted they couldn't sing, joined in.

This, our last, was the most convivial evening of all, as by now we felt we had got to know each other really well. There had been no time for small talk, and everybody had been able to share their very deepest concerns – in many cases, for the first time ever.

One of the problems with cancer, or, indeed, any serious illness, said Barbara, is that people tend to see themselves as "ill" and therefore unable to join in life to the full. They often won't go on holiday in case they get ill, they won't exercise in case they injure themselves, and they walk around in a wobbly, ill manner. The label "ill" tends to stick easily to people, and it's a label put on you both by your friends and family and by yourself. This can also mean that we breathe shallowly, as if constantly afraid, and this type of breathing sets up chemical imbalances to make us even more afraid. Thus it all becomes a vicious circle, and permanent panic can set in. Then we may become genuinely ill, just by thinking of ourselves as so.

The importance of proper breathing, especially for cancer patients, will be discussed in a later chapter, but for most of the residents on the course, the idea that breathing could have a profound effect on thought-processes, feelings and energy levels, made a dramatic impact.

By the end of the week, when we all said our rather tearful farewells, what were the most valuable aspects of the programme?

The first important thing people discovered, often to their surprise, was that the group itself supports people, and that patients get the experience of being strong and self-confident enough to ask for what they want. Group discussions of very serious issues also enabled patients to sort out their own priorities, feelings and sources of fear. The existence of the group, where everybody had the common experience of cancer, also enabled all to gain a clearer idea of where they were going, what they wanted and in which direction their lives may have to change.

For several, the concept of being able to sing your own song, to minister to your own needs rather than always to those of other people, was a new and heady one – and it can take time to adjust to the realisation that you as an individual are important, equally as important as anybody else. The experience of Bristol showed that self-transformation is possible, whatever your age, outlook, religion, education or social class.

Throughout the week, patients and their supporters – and me – all became aware that we are actually far stronger, far more special and also gentler and more compassionate than we may have thought. The emotions, sense of self-transformation and empowerment that came out during my week at Bristol are all, I'm told, common experiences on these programmes. Throughout the week, all these people who are facing a grave crisis – and cancer is often as serious for the supporters as for the actual patients – gradually discover their gentler selves, but at the same time become aware of their own strength and assertion. They become aware of the need to open up their hearts, let their guard down, to trust, to be unafraid – the lack of which may well predispose to cancer, and in any case definitely don't make things better once you've had a diagnosis.

The only sad aspect is that often it takes a severe crisis such as cancer to bring out the hidden strengths and talents which we all have.

Barbara said:

What people realise when they're here is that they are actually very special. Most come here imagining they are completely ordinary, of little account or importance, and they are surprised at what they can achieve once they are here. They become creative, they learn to trust the present moment.

On the final morning of the week, Friday, we did some more art therapy – this time in the relaxation room rather than the art room – and we were asked to represent an image of ourselves as we saw ourselves now, and as we would be when healed. Again, the pictures and images were all very different from each other. But, the important thing was that, by now, we were all able to imagine and portray ourselves as healed, whole people, serene and confident. Everybody agreed, when the pictures were shown and discussed, that serenity, confidence and wholeness were goals worth aiming at.

After the art therapy and its ensuing discussion, we got up in a circle to sing a New Age song as we went round the room touching hands and hugging people as we passed. There were few dry eyes in the room – some people said that such tears hadn't come to their eyes since they were children.

There was lunch on the final day and then we all said our fond, sad, emotional goodbyes. We had bonded very closely and strongly in the group and I felt very much one of them, even though I was not a patient, supporter, helper or therapist. It had been fun – there was a lot of dark humour present throughout the week and many jokes were cracked. Pat Pilkington said that humour was a very important healing tool, and we discussed the value of laughter therapy, now just catching on as a therapeutic ingredient for those suffering from chronic or serious illness.

By around half past two, most of us were on our way back home, to try and put the week's experience into practice in our everyday lives.

Patients who have been on such a week can attend a follow-up day, or another week, if they choose. We each took away leaflets, recipes and information which, at the beginning of the week, would probably have meant very little. Now, everybody was wholeheartedly enthusiastic about the Bristol programme, whereas at the beginning there was a large amount of suspicion and fear.

Nobody was led to expect that the treatments, therapies and healing on offer at Bristol would lead to a guaranteed cancer cure. The emphasis all the time was on how to live with it, how to cope with it, how to understand it so that the quality of life could be maintained and enhanced.

2

The Early Days

The modest-looking Centre in a British provincial town that was to influence cancer treatment and attitudes worldwide didn't start with the intention of being a cancer help centre. In fact, it didn't start with any specific intention at all.

The story goes back to the mid seventies when Canon Christopher Pilkington and his wife Pat moved to Bristol, when Christopher was appointed city rector. Always an unusual clergyman, Canon Pilkington came to feel that one of the most useful things the Christian ministry could do in a basically secular society was not to try to get people to come to church and hear the gospel, but to offer something much more practical – spiritual healing.

He had recognised healing abilities in himself, and felt the time had come to offer this generally to the people of Bristol. There was never any suggestion that he could heal the sick, like Jesus, nor were any great claims made. But the healing energy he seemed able to harness might, at the very least, make people feel better. Canon Pilkington realised that there is always a spiritual dimension to illness, something beyond the physical, and that when people feel better and stronger in themselves, this positive attitude very often helps to clear up the illness.

This is an ancient truth increasingly being recognised anew by the medical profession, but at the time, the height of the drug revolution, it was an unfashionable idea indeed. The prevailing attitude towards chronic illness at the time was that ever more powerful drugs would be able to combat every health problem, those of the mind as well as those of the body, as effective medication had helped to decimate deaths from infectious disease a few decades earlier.

Although at the time doctors mainly dismissed spiritual healing as much nonsense and quackery, no more than the power of suggestion at most, people started to flock to the healing ministry set up by the Pilkingtons. Originally conducted on church premises, the healing ministry grew so popular that it attracted not only the sick, but those in the healing professions as well. One of these was Penny Brohn, a sociologist who had recently trained as an acupuncturist, again at a time when acupuncture was widely regarded with deep suspicion. The healing ministry grew until there were about thirty part-time helpers, therapists and healers altogether – and it outgrew the temporary premises as well. It was felt that there was a desperate need to have a permanent centre where people could drop in and which would be open all the time for what is now known as the holistic approach.

Then, Canon Pilkington's father Guy died, leaving his son and daughter-in-law an unexpectedly large legacy. They knew exactly what they would do with it – set up a charitable foundation and buy suitable premises to continue the healing ministry. They bought a large house in Downfield Road, Bristol, and ever more people flocked to the centre. Whether they were actually healed of their complaints or not, they certainly felt much better. Here were people who actually cared, who healed with love and compassion, with the laying on of hands.

The atmosphere at the healing centre was quite unlike that of a doctor's surgery, where patients often feel nervous and frightened and, frequently, of little account. This was before the days of patient power and when the doctor, however incompetent, was regarded as the only repository of wisdom about health and illness. Also, the idea of restoring the whole person to health, and not just the part which had ceased to work efficiently, was in its infancy.

Then, in 1979, Penny Brohn herself contracted breast cancer. She was in her thirties, married with three young children, and her parents had both recently died. Everybody is surprised and devastated to get cancer and even though it is so very common, nobody really expects that the finger will point at them. She had for several years been aware not only of the powerful links between mind and body, between emotions and physical illness, but had been living, so far as possible, a healthy lifestyle, eating fresh, organic vegetables, becoming vegetarian and trying her best not to put toxic or polluted substances into her system. However, because of her double bereavement she was acutely aware of her vulnerability.

Her acupuncture training had taught her that, in order to remain healthy, our bodies have to be in harmony. In fact, acupuncture is designed to help the body regain its naturally harmonious state. So Penny was in the vanguard of the holistic health movement. How ironic that she, of all people, should get cancer.

Breast cancer was, and still is, the commonest form of cancer for women. This cancer strikes at the very heart of being a woman – at those secondary sex organs which are an integral part of a woman's femaleness and sexuality. Adornments and nurturers, female breasts have a deep-seated symbolic and practical significance. When they develop tumours, it's as if one's very femaleness is under malign attack.

Penny, in common with every other woman who develops a tumour in the breast, was overcome with panic, fear and anger. Her tumour was found to be malignant and a mastectomy was advised. But even in the midst of her terror, Penny felt there was something important that the tumour was telling her: that there was something wrong with her life, her attitudes, her emotions, which had caused her body cells to rise up in revolt and became cancerous. She knew that the body didn't start to attack itself without good reason, unless something had gone badly wrong. She felt she wanted to get to the bottom of the reasons why, as a young woman in her prime, she should have developed this disease.

Penny, whose story is told in her book *Gentle Giants*, experienced all the feelings common to those given a diagnosis of cancer – fear, terror, isolation, thoughts of why me, compounded with sensations of anger, guilt and panic. She wanted to heal herself, not with conventional medicine, but by trying to make her immune system strong so that it could fight the cancerous cells of its own accord. This is gradually being accepted by cancer doctors nowadays, but then it was new, unusual and seen as highly threatening to the medical profession. The attitude among cancer doctors and researchers was that, as so much money, time and resources were being put into cancer research worldwide, if diet, attitude or psychological factors made an appreciable difference, they would surely have been picked up by now.

So Penny did not find much sympathy among her doctors when she told them categorically, no, thank you, I don't want a mastectomy. I will try to get well in my own way. She describes in her book how teams of doctors came to see her in hospital to try to talk some sense into this difficult patient.

It is usual for newly-diagnosed cancer patients, even normally intelligent, articulate and assertive people, to become pathetically grateful for any mutilating or distressing treatment that may be offered. Penny Brohn was, and still is, unusual in that she knew this would not be the answer and that the way to get well would be to try and understand what had made her ill in the first place.

Penny exasperated her doctors so much that they told her the decisions would have to be taken out of her hands, as she was so clearly incoherent and uncooperative. The upshot was that she discharged herself from hospital after the biopsy and no clear idea of what to do next.

From her training in alternative medicine, her work at the healing ministry and her wide reading, Penny already knew that there were, in various parts of the world, doctors and practitioners treating cancer by unorthodox means, by diet, by "gentle" methods, by an understanding that cancer was a disease of the whole person and not just a few cells which had unaccountably gone out of control. These unorthodox cancer clinics accepted that the mind and spirit as well as the body had to be healed and that unless these aspects were taken into account, then the cancer would simply recur.

One of these unorthodox doctors was Josef Issels. His name became known to the British public only when the athlete Lillian Board, a cancer sufferer, had gone to his clinic in desperation, after conventional treatment had failed to arrest the march of the disease. She had died – and following this, three British cancer specialists went out to Germany to "investigate" the Issels clinic. They had found nothing of any value, and reported back as such.

Josef Issels, who had trained as a conventional doctor, and had worked in orthodox medicine for many years before coming to the conclusion that cancer was a whole-body, whole-mind disease, was castigated for having only a seventeen per cent cure rate for terminal patients. At the time, orthodox medicine could boast a one to two per cent cure rate for such patients – a figure which has not increased by even a fraction.

Penny mentioned to her doctor that she was thinking of going to the Issels clinic, notwithstanding his widespread vilification in the British press, and the doctor was scathing of him, snorting that in his opinion Issels was a charlatan.

Penny decided to go anyway, and bought tickets for herself and husband David, to spend a long weekend at the Ringberg Klinik at Bad Weissee in Bavaria. Her idea was simply to reconnoitre the place, to discover for herself whether there was anything of value in the treatments. She was to stay there for nine weeks.

One thing Penny learned while at the clinic was that, on the whole, patients turn to unorthodox treatments only after they have exhausted the gamut of conventional medicine, and when they have been told no more can be done. Penny was struck by how pale and ill most of the patients looked; they were, of course, terminal cases – or at least, cases which had been labelled terminal by their doctors.

Dr Issels surprised Penny by asking her if she knew why she had contracted the disease. She replied: yes, I think so. She was certain that the sudden, unexpected and premature deaths of both her parents had something to do with the development of the tumour. It was at the point where he told Penny that treatment of the body would be useless without an understanding of the psychological and spiritual factors involved, that she threw away her weekend ticket, decided to stay for as long as the treatment took, and despatched her husband back to Bristol, to look after the children in her prolonged absence.

The Issels clinic was expensive: in 1979, it cost around £100 a day, and Penny was able to pay for this only because of the legacy she had received from her parents. Otherwise, it would just not have been possible – and the Bristol Cancer Help Centre would probably never have come into existence.

The therapies which Dr Issels uses, some of which have been adopted and adapted by the Bristol Centre, will be explained in a later chapter. It is sufficient to say here that, although the treatments were perhaps not quite as "gentle" as proponents of the gentle approach seem to believe, they convinced Penny that, in the UK, a whole new attitude to cancer care was needed.

She came to understand that, in order to combat cancer, the body must be made stronger, and able to marshal its own defences against the disease. Although there is undoubtedly a place for surgery, chemotherapy and radiotherapy, these represent only part, and not the whole, of effective anti-cancer strategies. An important part of the Issels treatment was the right diet, one low in toxicity and easy to metabolise so that all available strength could go into fighting the cancer, rather than digesting toxic foods, or those which stay in the system for a long time, such as meat for example.

A large part of the diet consisted of raw fruits and vegetables. Penny, already used to eating raw food, didn't mind the diet, but found most of the other patients hated it.

One of Penny's many visitors during the nine long, lonely weeks of her treatment at the Issels clinic was Pat Pilkington, who arrived to keep her company and to bring her some warm clothes, as Penny had packed only enough for the initial weekend. Although ill both from her cancer – her left breast had not healed, and there was talk of a mastectomy at the Issels clinic – and from the treatments, Penny became fired with revolutionary zeal.

She said these memorable words to Pat Pilkington: "Together, we've got to change the world." She talked excitedly, feverishly, about her plans for setting up something like the Issels clinic in the UK. There was little like it available at all. The only other unorthodox cancer clinics were those in America, such as the Gerson and Hoxsey clinics, which themselves had suffered much adverse comment and accusations of charlatanism and quackery in the early days.

It was with these few words: we've got to change the world, that the Bristol Cancer Help Centre came into being. At the time, said Pat, she herself gave no serious thought to a cancer clinic. Her friend was desperately ill, in need of comfort and humouring, and had cooked up grandiose schemes out of her isolation, fear and also gratitude that the treatment she was receiving at the Issels clinic was definitely shrinking the tumour.

But the early days of the Bristol Centre were blessed with the kind of coincidence that must make even the most sceptical and cynical of individuals wonder whether, sometimes at least, there is an unseen hand at work. On the way home from the Bavarian clinic, Pat could not forget Penny's words. Of course, setting up a cancer clinic was impossible. None of the workers at Pilkington's healing ministry, who were all voluntary and part-time, knew anything about cancer. The premises themselves were unsuitable for cancer patients, many of whom might be too ill to make the journey to come for healing. None of them were doctors. There was no way to make it work.

Pat knew that if a cancer help centre with any credibility at all was to be set up, it had to be run by a doctor, somebody with impeccable credentials. As if by magic, almost before she had got her coat off on arriving home, that doctor appeared.

He was Alec Forbes, at the time a consultant physician at a hospital in Plymouth. Although not a cancer specialist as such, he had come to the conclusion that cancer was a disease of the mind, spirit and body. Alone among serious illnesses, Dr Forbes believed, it had the power to change people, to make them ask themselves searching questions about their lives, their attitudes, their purpose, their sense of self. Because it represents the most serious health crisis anybody can have – or did before the advent of AIDS – it forces thoughts on people which may not have been given any consideration before, such as their attitude towards death, towards their relationships, their work, their place in the world.

Dr Forbes, at the time four years off retirement, had become disillusioned after a professional lifetime in orthodox medicine, and he was looking for a new challenge. He had written to a clergyman colleague, asking if he knew of anybody undertaking radical work in the field of healing. This colleague wrote straight to the Pilkingtons, whom he knew, suggesting that perhaps they might like to meet Dr Forbes.

They met, and Pat outlined Penny Brohn's idea for a cancer centre which would take a completely new approach to the disease. At the time, 1980, a few, just a few, dissidents were starting to realise that cancer patients needed far more than orthodox treatment. They also needed loving care and a place to talk, and discuss their feelings, hopes and fears, without being shouted down or made to feel self-indulgent, or ungrateful for all the doctors were doing.

New approaches to cancer were, in fact, in the air. A retired army officer, Lieutenant-Colonel Marcus Macausland, had set up a charity looking at new approaches to serious illness, especially for cancer patients. In his home, he frequently ran healing sessions for cancer sufferers, where each would experience laying on of hands by professional spiritual healers. At the time, very few people with cancer ever spoke out about it – cancer was a word you could not mention.

At the same time, a group of medically qualified doctors were getting together to discuss holistic medicine, where the mind and spirit could be treated along with the body. Many people confuse holistic with alternative medicine, but there is a difference: holistic medicine does not dispense with orthodox treatments, but realises that for chronic disease at least, they may not be enough. It is not enough, with serious illness, just to treat the symptoms. We have to treat the whole person and have an understanding of the patient's individuality and uniqueness.

In America, the movement was already well on its feet, with doctors such as Carl and Stephanie Simonton, once completely orthodox, introducing the concept of visualisation for their cancer patients. At their clinic, patients were encouraged to visualise their cancer cells as weak and chaotic, being overcome by strong, powerful forces which patients themselves could marshal and imagine.

Penny Brohn was picking up on an avant-garde mood of the moment when she visualised this brave new cancer centre. But Penny needed Pat Pilkington to provide the practical input to Penny's seemingly wild ideas. She met Dr Forbes, the two of them clicked instantly, and he and his wife Norah decided to leave Plymouth and rent a modest flat in Bristol, so that the new cancer centre could come into being.

Dr Forbes had already carefully researched the relationship of diet to health, and had become convinced that very many people, given some simple lifestyle changes, could keep themselves well, or heal themselves from illness. He had been rather disappointed with the all too frequent reaction of patients when he told them that if they continued to smoke, drink, eat meat and never do any exercise, they would have to be on pills for the rest of their lives. When told this, the majority of patients would say: give me the pills, doctor.

Taking pills was easier than taking responsibility for your own health. Cancer, though, considered Dr Forbes, was different. Because of its random, chaotic and unpredictable nature, it aroused more fear than any other illness. Even those who knew little about cancer knew that if you cut out malignant cells from one part of the body, they could reappear at distant sites some time in the future. Whatever the treatment, however radical the surgery, you can never be sure you have beaten it.

So the cancer help centre was set up, initially at Downfield Road. It moved to Grove House, its present premises, in 1983. Residential weeks began in October 1983. Before that, patients stayed in local hotels for three-day courses.

Although from the first the Centre was intended to concentrate on spiritual healing, the founders had to work out very carefully which therapies would be on offer. Diet seemed especially important, as ever more evidence was coming to light that cancer, above all other diseases, was often intimately affected by diet. It was highly noticeable that people from the East, for instance, developed Western types of cancer when they started eating a Western diet.

It was also known that Seventh Day Adventists, who adhere to a strictly vegetarian diet which is also caffeine- and alcohol-free, contracted far less cancer than others in America. It was not clear how much this had to do with the diet, and how much to a strong belief in God's purpose, but their relatively cancer-free status was dramatic.

There would also have to be spiritual healing, relaxation, vitamin therapy, meditation and counselling at the new centre. Counselling is now generally seen as an important part of cancer treatment, even by the most orthodox doctors and hospitals, but in those days, the idea was startlingly new. In all, the Centre would provide a gently healing atmosphere, where cancer patients could be nurtured back to health at the same time as sampling these very different therapies and approaches.

The right doctor, the right therapies, the right approaches, presented themselves at the right time. And so did the right premises. When Pat and Penny realised that the Centre had to offer residential accommodation, they went looking for properties. They found a former convent in the Clifton area of Bristol, which already had, they felt, a spiritual atmosphere, and drew a deep breath and bought it with a bank loan.

An early problem was the question of a lift. The firm of architects hired by Pat and Penny said at an initial stage of the rebuilding that if they wanted a lift, it had to go in now. Penny had seen so many very ill patients at the Issels clinic to know that some at least would be incapable of climbing stairs, and so a lift was essential. The only drawback was that it was going to cost an extra £43,000 – money they simply didn't have.

Pat recalls that the magic which set the Centre in motion continued to bless them. On the very day they were wondering how they could possibly afford the lift, a cheque arrived for the exact amount, the whole £43,000.

From the first, the Centre attracted many supporters and helpers. In the early days, nobody was paid a salary of any kind, and well-wishers came to help at reception, the kitchen, to do the cleaning and other essential jobs. Staff changed shifts every two hours, and the whole thing seemed chaotic. There was little spare money, and for a time the Guy Pilkington Foundation, which Pat and her husband had set up with money left them by Christopher's father, picked up all the bills. But even with an entirely voluntary workforce, the bills mounted up.

From the start, the Centre attracted intense media interest. It seems likely that this was at least partly thanks to the personalities of the founders, Pat and Penny. Here were two "ordinary" women, not medically qualified, who had set up something very unusual. Both women are highly attractive, well-dressed, confident, outspoken, articulate individuals who went down well with the media.

Both believe that we have a purpose to serve in life, that we are here to sing our own song, to develop our own potential, and to pass on what we have learned to others. Neither Pat nor Penny ever set out to become famous, and neither could have foreseen that, before long, the Bristol Cancer Help Centre would become internationally known.

Although from the first, Bristol had attracted widespread media attention, two events were to catapult it into public consciousness for ever: the first was the opening in 1983 of the new residential centre by Prince Charles, at that time a staunch supporter of alternative medicine, and the other was a series of six BBC2 television programmes called *A Gentle Way with Cancer?*, put out the same year.

Out of the series of programmes came a book written by a radio journalist, Brenda Kidman, also called *A Gentle Way with Cancer*, and published by Century, then a new and go-ahead, but definitely mainstream, publishing house, in 1983. Brenda had been helped through her cancer crisis by Dr Ian Pierce (a colleague of Dr Alec Forbes) whom she met on Iona where he was conducting a retreat. She worked, with his help, on herself and then made a radio programme called *The Gentle Path* about her experience. While working on the programme she came to the Centre and interviewed Pat Pilkington.

The BBC2 series put Bristol on the map as never before. After the series was shown, the floodgates opened, and Bristol had to put itself on a more professional basis. All those who ran it were basically uncommercial, although well intentioned.

Bristol had to get itself on a firm financial footing. It also needed some staff who were not quite so temporary. That would mean two things: paying wages for permanent staff, and charging patients to go to Bristol. At first, everything had been free, but the cost of telephone calls, organic food, heating and lighting, and paying back the bank loan, was gradually bankrupting the Centre.

Patients who came either on a day or residential basis began to be charged for their accommodation and treatment, although there were always bursary funds available for those who could not pay. They did not want to turn anybody away for lack of funds. They also set about serious fund-raising.

By 1984, it seemed as though the Bristol Cancer Help Centre was on an extremely firm footing. Dr Alec Forbes, the medical director, had instituted a holistic mind, body and spirit regime which consisted of a mainly vegan, raw food diet with vitamin and mineral supplements; relaxation and visualisation therapies, spiritual healing and counselling. The Centre was fully booked for many months ahead, and Pat and Penny had gathered round them a dedicated, professional staff, both lay helpers and specialist therapists, who were working to provide a safe, loving and healing environment whereby desperately ill cancer patients, or those struggling to come to terms with an unexpected cancer diagnosis, would be enabled to face life with positivity, joy and love for as long as they had got.

Bristol has been called an "alternative clinic", but it has never set itself up in opposition to the orthodox cancer world. From the start, it has been concerned to work in conjunction with conventional doctors, so that the two approaches should come together to provide the best possible care for cancer patients.

Thanks partly to the television programmes and the books, also the willingness of Pat and Penny to give interviews and speak in public, Bristol gradually gained in credibility. People from all walks of life came and benefited from the variety of gentle therapies on offer. But the six-part series, which had done so much to put Bristol on the international map as a unique, very special place, almost caused its destruction seven years later.

The producer of the series, Ann Paul, was highly enthusiastic about Bristol. At first, she had intended to do only one forty-minute programme, but as she researched the subject, it became clear that this short space of time would not give the "gentle" method a fair chance. Patients had to be filmed, not only at the Centre, but when leading their ordinary lives later. Because if they were unable to put the Bristol message into practice in their everyday lives, it would have an extremely limited usefulness. The idea, then, was to follow a number of patients with cancer for several weeks.

No programmes like this had ever been made by a television company before. But following the reviews in the Sunday papers after the first programme's transmission, heavy pressure was brought on the controllers to axe the series. In the end, however, they agreed to show all six on condition there would be a live studio discussion after the final programme was transmitted.

Chaired by Michael Dean, the panel consisted of Brenda Kidman, Dr Dick Richards, maverick doctor and author of the book *Topic of Cancer*, and doctors Walter Bodmer, Tim McElwain and Ian McColl, all cancer specialists.

The panel of doctors was less obviously hostile to Bristol than many doctors of orthodox medicine might be. They said they were very moved by the programmes, and they highlighted the severe failures of orthodox doctors to establish fruitful relationships with their cancer patients, or to understand what they might be going through.

Dr Tim McElwain made the very fair point that it was important when attempting to assess unorthodox therapies, to make a distinction between the effect on the cancer and the effect on the patient. At the moment, he said, there was no evidence whatever that "gentle" therapies influenced the outcome of cancer in any measure whatever. Dr Ian McColl said that while anything which boosted the patients' morale was clearly of benefit, there was a definite lack of evidence to support the hypothesis that these therapies made any difference.

These views were reiterated by Walter Bodmer, of the Imperial Cancer Research Fund (ICRF). Dr Dick Richards, himself a fairly unorthodox medic, made the plea for funds to become available so that the Bristol approach could be properly tested. All the orthodox cancer specialists kept asking for evidence, because unless this was present, what Bristol was offering, however well intentioned, was gobbledegook.

And so the panel began to discuss the feasibility of setting proper trials in motion. All were agreed that there was no evidence that what a person ate could eliminate the cancer, even though such claims had often been made. But they equally agreed that nobody could be certain about diet or any other of the therapies until they had been tested in proper trials.

Brenda Kidman became enthusiastic about the possibility of scientific trials – she, like many cancer patients, had been right through the orthodox mill before going to Bristol, and on the programme it was agreed that steps would be taken to set the study in motion. The diet was the easiest aspect of the Bristol treatment to study; the effects of spiritual healing, relaxation, massage and so on, were more problematic.

It seemed a happy enough outcome to the debate: for the first time ever, orthodox and unorthodox specialists would be working in harmony, setting in motion a trial which would, the Bristol people were convinced, prove to the world that their methods worked.

The Bristol Cancer Help Centre had never claimed that it could cure cancer. It had never made any specific claims at all. Neither did it at any time advise patients to discontinue with their orthodox treatment when on the programme. Some patients did decide to go it alone, but this was their choice. Many others felt that their cancers needed both approaches, and decided to stick with their chemotherapy or radiotherapy.

Clearly, Bristol was convinced that people with cancer derived dramatic benefit from the combination of gentle approaches, otherwise they would not continue to be in business. Equally clearly, the patients who attended Bristol were certain that it had changed their lives. Most spoke of "before Bristol" and "after Bristol", as they felt that going to the cancer centre gave them a completely new outlook on life, a new attitude and the opportunity and courage to change what was not working. Many patients said that they now saw where they had been blind before.

For their part, the Bristol workers were certain they were offering something of value, but how much better if they could gain genuine credibility with a scientific evaluation. They were only too eager to co-operate with the Cancer Research Campaign and the ICRF, which eventually agreed to set a study in motion, where Bristol patients would be compared with those having only orthodox treatments, over a period of five years. This study, the Bristol staff were certain, would give them the standing they were seeking in the scientific world, and enable their dream of conventional and unconventional treatments working hand-in-hand to come true.

In the meantime, as the study got under way, Bristol became ever more popular, and attracted ever more patients. Penny and Pat were invited to speak at many international venues, and more books began to appear about the Centre's work.

The first book to appear after Brenda Kidman's was Dr Alec Forbes' *The Bristol Diet*. He was to stay at the Centre as medical director for four and a half years, during which time his wife Norah died. Then he felt it was time to move on – but by now idealistic young doctors were clamouring to go to Bristol.

Penny Brohn wrote two books about Bristol: *Gentle Giants*, and *The Bristol Programme*. Books on Bristol's dietary regime also appeared, and Dr Rosy Thomson, who later joined the Centre, wrote a book called *Loving Medicine*, which consisted of moving case histories of those who had been to Bristol. Not all survived, but all felt that the quality of their lives had improved immeasurably for the Bristol input.

It seemed the Centre could do no wrong. Everybody loved it. The press flocked down to write articles about the place, and to talk to the founders and doctors there.

Then, in September 1990, the blow fell. It was stated in a bald press release issued by the Imperial Cancer Research Fund (ICRF) that breast cancer patients who had gone to Bristol were two to three times more likely to die than those just having the orthodox treatment.

Could it be true? Could Bristol's guardian angels, who had watched over and blessed the Centre for so many years, be deserting them?

3

Scandal!

The scandal that overtook Bristol in September 1990 is so complicated, so multi-layered that even now, when so much of it has been picked over, it remains difficult to disentangle. The steps that set the study in motion were initiated, as we have seen, by the BBC2 series which was broadcast in 1983.

Initially, the directors were proud and delighted that the Centre, a small, unassuming, provincial complementary healing centre, should have been the focus of so much serious and mainly adulatory media attention. But "Bristol" – as it came to be universally known – had from its earliest days appeared charmed and blessed – the right people had appeared, the right premises, the right publicity. In gathering its programme together, Bristol had taken what seemed to be the best, at the same time as the most radical, complementary approaches to cancer, at a time when these were new and exciting, and certainly newsworthy.

Although a few "alternative" cancer clinics had existed at least since the 1940s in various parts of the world, they had always seemed exotic and unreachable to the majority, as well as somewhat questionable and peculiar. The notion of using such treatments as coffee enemas, mistletoe therapy, visualisation, to help cancer patients get well again did not widely appeal. Bristol had by no means invented different approaches to cancer, but had collected the best of them from all over the world and put them, for the first time, into a complete package.

Bristol had credibility, it had gravitas. Also, whatever the orthodox world might think, the patients loved it. They loved the care, the attention, the nurturing. Even when Bristol started charging, people still flocked to the Centre. Given such adulation by cancer patients, given the growing interest by some of the more avant-garde members of the orthodox medical world, given that an increasing number of idealistic young doctors wanted to come to Bristol to learn all about its methods, it seemed as if they were floating on the crest of a wave.

Already the Centre had become world-famous, already Pat Pilkington and Penny Brohn were in demand at international conferences on cancer care and complementary medicine, and already "Bristol" had become a word to be reckoned with in cancer treatments. To add to its credibility, Bristol had never set itself up in competition with the orthodox medical establishment: it was, from the first, purely a place where cancer patients could get extra help, tender loving care, at the same time as continuing, if they wished, with their conventional treatments.

Some patients appeared to experience miraculous remissions from a visit to Bristol. But what they found, above all, was that the programme increased their self-awareness, enabled them to lessen their fear, and to improve the quality of their lives. It seemed as if Bristol was destined to go on from strength to strength, that it had a very firm base, and nothing could go wrong.

In view of all this, the report which appeared in *The Lancet* on 8 September, 1990, was a bombshell.

The report, supposed to be "interim" rather than the last word on the subject, was dismissive in its description of Bristol and its methods, also of "alternative" methods generally in the treatment of cancer. The abstract, in bold type at the beginning of the paper, stated:

> The Bristol Cancer Help Centre . . . attracted much public interest and profound medical scepticism.

The report, which became known as "the Chilvers report" after one of its authors, Professor Clair Chilvers, the others being F. S. Bagenal, D. F. Easton, E. Harris and Professor Tim McElwain, was highly questioning of Bristol throughout.

The introduction to the paper stated: "Interest in and use of alternative methods and practices for the treatment of cancer has been growing for several years despite lack of any scientific evidence for anti-tumour effects. Most cancer specialists are not happy to recommend 'alternative' therapy, although some take the view that it is at least harmless."

It went on to say:

> Alternative cancer regimens tend to be based on three notions – that "detoxification" leads to a better quality of life and possible cancer regression (this being the basis of the many diets supposed to have an anti-tumour effect); that the immune system can be stimulated and that this will lead to an anti-tumour effect; and that a holistic approach, seeking a harmonious balance between the patient's mind, body, and spirit, will be beneficial.

Readers of the report were left in little doubt as to the outcome of the study, begun in 1986. The results showed that survival rates of breast cancer patients attending Bristol were "significantly poorer" than those of the controls.

The report, which was four pages long and represented the main study in *The Lancet* that week, concluded unequivocally:

> . . . . the possibility that some aspect of the BCHC regimen is responsible for [their] decreased survival must be faced. For example, does radical adherence to a stringent diet shorten life in patients whose survival is already threatened by cancer? Our study certainly shows that patients choosing to attend the BCHC do not gain any substantial survival benefit. Whether quality of life is enhanced is yet to be answered. Other alternative practitioners should have the courage to submit their work to this type of stringent assessment.

The authors then thanked the BCHC staff and hospital consultants for their "generosity" and "prompt response" to the survey.

The media, all of which gave the story headline coverage, were astonished – but few thought to question whether it was likely that gentle therapies could actually hasten death – or that the Bristol regime made patients significantly more ill than orthodox therapies, all of which were greatly feared for their many and known adverse side-effects.

Dr Myles Harris, writing in the *Evening Standard* on Thursday 6 September, 1990 – two days before the survey was officially published, although there had been a massive press conference the day before – was clearly confused and surprised that Bristol treatments could have a deleterious effect – but, like most others, he never questioned the validity of the study, suggesting that the holistic movement must now be willing to throw "untested, well-meaning assumptions overboard in favour of facts". Most other papers and journalists did not question the possibility that there might be something seriously the matter with the study. Mary Kenny, writing in the *Sunday Telegraph*, said confidently:

> The experts may be baffled, but I am not. It seems to me that people who go on diets of raw and partly cooked vegetables, beans, pulses and carrot juice can become seriously unwell if they haven't got cancer: if they have cancer as well, they will – in my view – become seriously worse, quicker . . . Meat is health; our very bones have been bred on it. Vegetarianism is, for the most part, unhealthy.

Mary, an astute and popular journalist, voiced, perhaps unthinkingly, the prejudices and attitudes which had lain only just below the surface all those years. While on the surface praising Bristol for the help it was giving to cancer patients, most sections of the media took unashamed delight in describing just how "weird" the therapies were, just how suspicious they remained of holistic treatment. It took only one adverse finding to bring down the whole edifice with a crash. Britain had, as a nation, not really been open to the holistic message. Mary Kenny, in common with most reporters writing about the Bristol affair, had herself made no study of cancer treatments or patients, either orthodox or alternative; she knew little in depth about the Bristol programme, and appeared not to have spoken to any of the patients who felt they had benefited.

In an interview with the *Independent*, Professor Clair Chilvers of Nottingham University, who co-ordinated the study, was reported as saying:

> We were not expecting such a clear-cut result. It led us to re-check both the computer and our input into it for mistakes. We even re-checked against the original case notes.

Professor Tim McElwain was less circumspect, saying that there was not a jot of evidence that special diets helped to stop the spread of cancer.

The Bristol staff, patients and helpers were stunned. They had co-operated at every stage with the ICRF and CRC people, fully believing that their methods would be vindicated. After all, they had been extremely enthusiastic about the study, realising the need to have their methods assessed and investigated, so that they would have both evidence, as well as a gut feeling, that their therapies were actually helping cancer patients.

The effect of *The Lancet* paper at the Centre was swift and unequivocal. Patients who had already booked a day or a week cancelled, and bookings dramatically slowed down. People who for so many years had flocked to Bristol, and blessed it, now deserted it in droves. Not only that, but other cancer-help centres, counselling centres and complementary clinics suddenly found themselves bereft of patients.

The Royal London Homoeopathic Hospital, which had been running a complementary service for several years, on the NHS, for cancer patients, discovered that patients stopped coming. At one fell swoop, as it seemed, complementary therapies of all kinds were completely discredited.

One wonders what would have happened if *The Lancet* had printed a paper which said that chemotherapy or radiotherapy dramatically shortened life. It is unlikely that it would have been so universally and uncritically accepted. Had the report found that Bristol breast cancer patients were two to three times more likely than others to survive, would the story have attracted such coverage? It is unlikely.

Although the media unquestioningly accepted the validity of the findings, many Bristol supporters and doctors instantly rallied round, questioning the statistics and asking whether this really could be the case. It seemed impossible to believe that more than a decade of gentle help and care could be swept away in an instant by a damaging report.

As the story took hold, some reporters and commentators went further, denigrating the whole self-help, counselling movement which had been gradually growing, and which was to some extent spearheaded by the existence of the Bristol Centre. The attempts by Bristol staff, patients and sympathetic doctors to turn the tide had little initial effect. That one report, those interim findings, had been almost enough to shatter the whole delicate edifice of alternative and complementary care.

Tim Sheard, one of the Centre's doctors, claimed that the interim report – it was never intended to be the last word on the subject – had omitted vital information, such as that some of the Bristol patients had been far more ill than the controls. In other words, they were not comparing like with like. Nor was any analysis made of the data supplied by the patients in replies to annual questionnaires, documenting whether or not they actually followed any of the regimes such as the diet, the vitamins, healing or counselling. Some had attended the Centre for one day only – and may not have altered their lives in the slightest.

It wasn't long, however, before a few scientists and doctors began to look at the figures a little more closely, and criticise the way the Bristol survey had been undertaken. Professor Karol Sikora, who had been favourably impressed by a visit to the Centre, collaborated with Centre therapists to find an effective way of introducing appropriate complementary therapies at his Hammersmith Hospital oncology department. He said on record that the paper was fundamentally flawed, as like was not being compared with like.

In calling the report a "fiasco", Professor Sikora added that differences between the extreme factions of orthodox and complementary medicine had been highlighted. Nowhere in the report did it state that Bristol patients had abandoned their orthodox medical treatment – which in fact was maintained by both Bristol patients and controls. This should have alerted astute readers to the possibility of something being wrong. Bristol was always a help centre, not an alternative clinic such as the Issels and Gerson clinics, whose regimes were intended to replace orthodox cancer treatments with a completely different approach.

The *Lancet* study gave rise to a whole spate of letters to the journal once people had had the chance to read the paper in its entirety, and see where it might have gone wrong. A group of researchers from the London School of Hygiene and Tropical Medicine commented on the "extremely odd" nature of a number of the findings. A very long letter in the same issue – 10 November, 1990 – by Professor Clair Chilvers and her co-authors, commented: "We regret that our paper has created the widespread impression that the CHC regimen directly caused the differences that we observed in recurrence and survival." This was never stated, they maintained, and added that it was much more likely that the differences could be explained by the increased severity of disease in the Bristol patients (which was in fact the case).

But the damage had been done, not only because of the widespread and hysterical press coverage, with headlines such as "Double death threat at veggie clinic" but because of the negative tone in the original paper. The references to "scepticism", "unproven therapies" and the possibility that the diet could have caused patients to relapse were stated unequivocally, either in the original paper, or at the press conference which preceded its publication in *The Lancet*.

By the middle of November 1990, though, the scientists were admitting that they might have made errors in their study. Bristol in the meantime remained devastated. Their waiting lists had shrunk to nothing, and the uneasy alliance between orthodox and complementary therapies which had been gradually growing all through the 1980s, now seemed shattered for ever.

Tim Sheard, the Centre's representative at the time, called on the Chilvers team to retract their paper in its entirety, which they refused to do. Professor Tim McElwain now seemed to be suffering from a crisis of confidence. Originally he had said at the press conference that he would not now recommend a patient to go to Bristol, and he had wholeheartedly condemned the rigid diet. Now he himself was admitting that perhaps the study was not as good as it could have been. McElwain was now saying: "It seems unlikely that if you go to Bristol it will do you harm."

There is still a lot of confusion and dissatisfaction surrounding the premature publication of that Bristol paper and many theories abound. Some commentators, such as Martin J. Walker, author of the book *Dirty*

Medicine, believes it was all a conspiracy to denigrate natural medicine. His view is that Bristol, along with a number of other complementary clinics, was targeted by HealthWatch, a "quackbusting" organisation, who, according to Martin Walker, wanted to close them down and so limit patient choice in healthcare. Walker believes, after three years' painstaking research for his book, that orthodox medicine is increasingly feeling threatened by complementary therapies, partly because patients like them so much, partly because they might make people question the orthodox treatments – certainly there have been few conspicuous successes recently in the treatment of cancer – and partly because if enough people turned to alternative methods, the multinational drug companies would soon be out of business.

There seems little doubt that, whether or not most supporters of complementary medicine would go quite so far as Martin Walker, there is a deep-seated hostility to alternative methods of medical care among many sections of the medical profession, even though, throughout the 1980s, therapies such as relaxation, visualization, massage and aromatherapy had been increasingly assimilated into hospital care, particularly for terminal patients. Hospices, especially, have led the way in promoting holistic care to add to the quality of life for seriously ill patients who are not expected to recover.

Although Professor Chilvers and others involved in the report partially retracted their findings only two months after publication of the study, the damage was done, almost permanently.

Stories began to appear in the medical and lay press that patient demand for the Bristol treatment had virtually disappeared – and indeed many of their patients, doctors, therapists and staff had deserted; a number of "first person" stories by patients drew attention to the difficulties of the diet, the expense of the vitamin and mineral supplements, and the uncertainty as to whether any of these regimes would make the slightest difference to the cancer.

The overwhelming feeling the public was left with, after scores of articles, news bulletins, letters to medical journals, was that, even if Bristol were not actually harmful as had originally been stated, it didn't do much positive good.

Then, shockingly, Professor Tim McElwain, who had publicly cast doubt on the Bristol programme, committed suicide by slashing his throat in his bathroom. Professor McElwain, consultant physician at the Royal Marsden Hospital, was fifty-three years old, at the top of his profession and well respected in the orthdox cancer world. He was said to have been subject to bouts of depression for some time – before the publication of the Chilvers report.

Professor McElwain's suicide raises several questions, most of which could be answered only by him. Was he out to get Bristol, and close it down? Why did he have such a down on the diet? Why did he, and the other authors of the report, rush into print before the research project was finished and proper checks were made on the statistics?

The Bristol founders and staff were hoping that the partial retraction of the Chilvers paper and the public messages of support would restore their pre-Chilvers situation. However, two women, Isla Bourke and Heather Goodare, both cancer patients who had been to Bristol, and whose data were used in the survey, weren't so sure. They felt that nothing less than a retraction of the whole study, from beginning to end, would restore Bristol's fortunes and renew public confidence in the complementary therapies they both felt had changed their lives for the better.

Isla, who had worked for most of her life in the tourist industry, and Heather, an academic editor turned counsellor, got together to form the Bristol Survey Support Group, most of whose members were women who had taken part in the survey as research subjects. The aims of the BSSG when formed were, in Heather's words, "to share feelings and experiences, to promote research into complementary therapies, to debate the ethical issues arising for patients, and to consider what further action, if any, might be appropriate".

After discussion with members, the agenda extended to, first, getting the survey stopped and, second, securing a full retraction of the report. A year after the Chilvers report – a year which had shown Bristol in no uncertain terms that patients' confidence in the therapies had taken a severe knock and was not returning – the BSSG wrote a letter to *The Lancet* and sent out a press release which stated their aims.

They wanted an investigation by an independent body – the Charity Commission – into the continued funding of research which had already been shown to be fundamentally flawed. They wanted the researchers to admit publicly that their findings were invalid, and should be withdrawn; they wanted an apology to be made to the distraught women who took part in the survey, who had not been informed by the researchers that the study was now at an end, and for the remainder of the research grant to be given to Bristol, to fund its own research projects.

There were also other important questions they wanted publicly answered: why was the protocol not regularly reviewed by the Ethics Committee of the Royal Marsden Hospital? Why was the promised "quality of life" study not carried out?

Further questions remained unanswered, and the BSSG pressed on. On 2 April, 1992, the group had its first significant success: they broadcast on Channel Four a *Free for All* programme, *Cancer Positive*, where their complaints were aired to a wide audience. The most telling remark was that the women recruited for the survey had been used as pawns. Isla Bourke said at the time: "Nobody expected the pawns to fight back, but we did because we didn't want this to happen in the future."

The Channel Four film and subsequent publicity caused a great deal of embarrassment for Britain's two main cancer charities who had funded the study, the Imperial Cancer Research Fund and the Cancer Research Campaign. Sir Walter Bodmer – who was on the original 1983 studio panel discussing the Bristol approach – and Professor Gordon McVie could not satisfactorily answer the questions put by the increasingly insistent Isla Bourke and Heather Goodare.

Heather Goodare asked: "If you read in the newspaper that if you went to Bristol you were twice as likely to die and that your cancer was three times as likely to recur, would you go to such a place?" She went on: "When you saw the report of the study, what did you think of it?"

Sir Walter Bodmer admitted that he had been extraordinarily surprised and very concerned. To Heather's next question: "What did you do?" he replied that he got advice on it. Isla then asked him if he had passed the report, to which Sir Walter said that he had no control over whether the work was published or not.

Clearly the cancer charities hoped that the affair would blow over. But they reckoned without the BSSG, who stated that they would not be satisfied until they gained a full retraction. The cancer charities had been made to look silly, at the very least, and there was no way they could wriggle out of it.

All this time, Bristol itself continued to fight for its life. The Centre faced bankruptcy as their patient numbers did not increase, in spite of many glowing letters of support in the press. It was a grim time for Bristol, and a grim time generally for unorthodox cancer therapies. The Centre therefore appointed a number of scientists, doctors and researchers to advise them and help them to be as ground-breaking in the nineties as they had been in the eighties. But, do what they might, the ghost of the Chilvers report continued to cling round them, and Isla Bourke and Heather Goodare knew it.

Their opinion was that a full and complete public retraction of the Chilvers paper was essential. Bristol had, from the first, been committed to the "gentle way" and it was founded by people with strong spiritual principles and belief in the fundamental goodness and positivity of human nature. Isla and Heather, more objectively, knew that strong tactics had to be adapted to get the report withdrawn.

In January 1994 the Charity Commission finally sent out a press release to say that it had carried out its own enquiry into the conduct of the cancer charities at the request of the BSSG, and upheld the group's complaint. The study had been funded by the Imperial Cancer Research Fund and the Cancer Research Campaign, and was carried out by the Institute of Cancer Research, all separate but strongly linked organisations. The Charity Commission finally found that the ICRF and the CRC both failed to exercise proper supervision of the research project, and did not take the necessary steps to ensure that the research was soundly based. Its report did not mention that the study reported the results of only two years' work, when it was always supposed to be a five-year study. Although this story did not receive quite the widespread coverage of the original survey, it was enough to turn the tide back in Bristol's favour. Bookings at the centre picked up and previous patients returned.

By June 1992, eighteen months before the Charity Commission castigated the cancer charities, Bristol felt recovered enough to hold a press conference at which most of the television and radio stations were present where "the way forward" would be announced. Several doctors and academics who had continually pledged their support for Bristol were present, including Professor Karol Sikora, one of the most open-minded and forward-thinking of modern oncologists.

In charge of the oncology department at Hammersmith Hospital, Professor Sikora said at this conference that he instituted some "Bristol" regimes into his cancer care programme in 1989. "I had expected Bristol to be cranky, but found it made complete sense," he said, and added:

It is a false notion that Bristol represents some cranky alternative. I hope that the lessons we have learned from the Bristol tragedy will enable us to merge holistic with orthodox cancer care over the next few years. High technology treatment and research is expensive, whereas holistic care is relatively cheap. I see big changes over the next ten years, and one of the greatest of these will be to integrate holistic cancer therapies within the NHS.

The next speaker at the conference was Dr Michael Weir, a former Director of Community Medicine for Wirral District, and a pioneer in introducing holistic concepts into the NHS. He is not a cancer specialist, but a community doctor. He said:

The holistic concept is slowly becoming part of mainstream medicine. The Bristol way of understanding illness involves upheaval, and a reappraisal of your whole lifestyle. There have been enormous increases in cancer this century, and the diagnosis of cancer is terrifying. Also, the treatments are frightening. Cancer is an illness above all others which is demoralising to a person's well-being, and the NHS has been guilty of neglecting this aspect.

The Centre itself developed as a protest against the inadequacies of standard NHS care (we have already heard about Penny Brohn's struggle with orthodox specialists). Bristol offers, above all, a philosophy of hope. One of the greatest problems with cancer, apart from the physical toll, is that it brings great fear and distress which drains the body and makes it even less able to fight the illness. I believe that the Bristol Centre should remain radical, and that it's up to orthodox medicine to show that their methods work. Double-blind trials will never work to evaluate cancer treatments, as it is such an unpredictable disease.

At this same press conference, Bristol announced that it had come to the conclusion that some dramatic changes had to be set in motion. Mobile teams would be set up to visit people in other parts of the country; in other words, Bristol would become less inward-looking. They would also set up a database to monitor the nutritional and other therapies, and they would form closer links with hospitals, universities and regional cancer organisations, integrating more with the cancer care set-up generally.

The Chilvers report, as the report has come to be christened, but officially known as the Bristol Study, was a transformational experience for Bristol itself. Reluctantly, Bristol staff had come to the conclusion that there were people who were happy to see them done down, that it was easier to believe bad news – even when a minute's reflection would have led people seriously to question the apparent bad news – and that they were fragile, rather than strong.

Although some people believed that the Bristol message had now been assimilated into cancer care generally, the Centre felt that its work was by no means finished. There was still no centre exactly like it anywhere else in the world, still no residential clinic dealing specifically with cancer in England where people could learn about themselves and explore the deepest recesses of their being in safety and confidence, at the same time as taking part in therapies which were enjoyable and unaggressive, such as art and music therapy, group counselling and discussions, and relaxation and meditation. The Bristol board of directors felt that the Centre should remain a concentrated source of a different approach to cancer, but that, in order to remain strong and credible, they had to forge even closer links with the community.

Penny Brohn decided to leave the Centre after working there for twelve years. She had originally intended to stay for ten but felt that, owing to the Chilvers report and the dramatic happenings since, she could not leave until it was back on its feet. The impact of the report and its aftermath had a serious effect on Penny – her cancer returned. It was a time of enormous stress for all Bristol staff, especially when their doctors and therapists kept leaving.

Penny's responsibilities were taken over by Pat Pilkington, who, although a close colleague and friend of Penny's, had remained rather in the background while Penny took centre stage. Pat was now to be the chief spokeswoman for the Centre and the woman who would take it fighting and strong into the nineties and beyond.

The aftermath of the Chilvers report enabled Bristol to realise that it was, above all, a centre for spiritual change. The diet and the therapies undoubtedly helped towards self-realisation, but the message had to go much deeper than that if any genuine, long-lasting transformation could be made.

It is a great tribute to the Bristol staff that they were able to be open-minded enough to realise that certain changes were necessary, that their work had to move into a new phase. But they accept that it is unlikely that Bristol would still be in operation without the tireless work and campaigning of the Bristol Survey Support Group. Without their work, and without the conviction of Isla Bourke and Heather Goodare that the publication of the Chilvers report had to be investigated by an independent body, it is almost certain that Bristol would have had to close, obliterated in an avalanche of adverse but completely unwarranted publicity.

Isla and Heather did not rest until they had achieved their goal: the vindication of the Bristol Centre. The existence and campaigning ability of the BSSG is the clearest example yet of patient power. It shows what can be done when people are convinced that there has been a great injustice.

The Chilvers report has still not been formally withdrawn, but the record has been corrected, and the Editor of *The Lancet*, Robin Fox, has been quoted by the Editor of the *British Medical Journal* as saying that after he dies the words "Bristol Cancer Help Centre" will be found tattooed on his heart.[1]

[1] Smith, R. 'Charity Commission censures British cancer charities'. *BMJ* 1994; 308: 155–6 (15 January).

4

Bristol After Chilvers

Perhaps the most important lesson that the staff of Bristol Cancer Help Centre learned from the traumatic aftermath of the Chilvers report was that they were, far more than they could ever have realised previously, isolated and potentially vulnerable. They were also, perhaps, rather naive, in the way that many complementary and unorthodox clinics often are. Fired with revolutionary zeal, with a conviction that they have something special or different to offer, complementary clinics can often be blinded to the fact that others offering more conventional or standard treatment may be resentful and hostile. In a sense, complementary clinics can fling off the boring, uncomfortable, orthodox treatment for an enticing mixture of love, nurture, affection, massage and counselling. Patients given up for lost, for dead, often returned from Bristol with a new youth, vigour and vitality. Also, of course, many of them fell in love with Bristol, with its therapies, its approaches, even its diet. No wonder some in the orthodox world, battling unsuccessfully for so many years against this dread disease, became jealous.

Compared to standard general hospitals, Bristol appeared seductive and alluring, offering as it did a heady mixture of mind and body therapies. Bristol realised this, and it was one reason why it was keen to co-operate with the major cancer charities, so that they could join forces.

Bristol gradually came to the realisation that by collaborating with the big cancer charities, it had unwittingly taken part in and even helped to bring about its near downfall. It took the concerted efforts of the Bristol Survey Support Group, those who were grateful but whose lives were not intimately tied up with the Centre, to be able to see what had really happened, and take determined steps to prevent further damage. The incident also forced Bristol to reappraise its own treatment and approaches, and see what could be done to make its work as relevant, as pioneering, as avant-garde, in the nineties as it had been in the eighties.

It gradually became clear that if Bristol were to survive, and carry on to expand its work, it was imperative to forge links with the wider world, not perhaps only in the field of orthodox cancer treatments, but in the rapidly growing sphere of holistic care generally.

It was equally important to become attached to mainstream sources of cancer care, where these were sympathetic with the Bristol approach, to work together rather than in the somewhat uneasy alliance of the past, where there had been at best a grudging appreciation of the work, and always thinly veiled hostility beneath the surface.

There are, of course, no easy answers to cancer: some people recover, others die. Some tumours are fast-growing, whereas others can live in symbiosis with their hosts for years. Some cancers are more dangerous, more life-threatening than others. But we may be ill-advised to put all of our faith in mainstream medicine to deal with a disease as little understood as cancer. We have had enough false hopes over the years for scepticism to be widespread; yet it is not. It is common to announce a wonderful new drug for this or that serious chronic illness, long before it has come on to the market, and to wheel a few "successes" on to a public platform from early trials. Sometimes, these orchestrated "breakthroughs" are appeals for more funds in disguise. If we could only complete the research, the PR material goes, we could cure many more people. The cure depends on YOU, we are told as we are asked to dig deep into our pockets to fund the "vital" research. We continue to place a pathetic faith in the orthodox system to find remedies and cures to come to our rescue.

Few of these excitedly announced new drugs ever live up to early expectations. But the underlying idea behind conventional medicine remains: that without any input (other than perhaps financial) from you, the wonderful new drugs, which will be available in five years' time, will do the trick.

Conventional, orthodox medicine is big business. It is multi-national, it pays its top people very high salaries. It costs you, the patient, a lot of money, whether this comes direct, from taxation, or from insurance schemes. Conventional medicine is highly expensive, the drugs and treatments are costly and it is often paternalistic. It makes little allowance for individuality and, as yet, orthodox medicine can only treat the symptoms, not the underlying cause. This is not to ignore its value. Sometimes, with cancer, surgery is required – a fungating mass is unlikely to go away with only positive thinking and a low-toxicity diet. But where conventional medicine works best is with acute complaints. Surgery can deal effectively with a hernia, with a burst appendix, with accidents, burns and bodily obstructions. Pills can treat acute infections.

But even when orthodox medicine can treat the presenting condition successfully, it often forgets that every illness, whether serious or minor, has a mental or emotional component. The emotional impact of an illness is in direct relation to its longevity: most of us soon get over the depression caused by flu, as flu itself is a self-limiting infection. But we cannot expect that surgery, chemotherapy or radiation, however successful they may appear to be, will in themselves enable us to emotionally "get over" a diagnosis of cancer.

There is a place for both high-tech and loving treatments; one type of medicine will never entirely supplant the other, and in order to offer the best type of care, they must work in harmony.

What is now known as complementary medicine comes from a much older and gentler healing tradition than scientific approaches. It is now generally accepted that self-help groups, counselling, relaxation, visualisation and body therapies such as massage can be invaluable for the well-being of cancer patients, yet before Bristol came into existence, there were no such notions in standard cancer wards. The importance of addressing psychological implications of cancer were hardly considered. Patients were rarely told they had cancer and, when they were, they were expected to suffer in silence, not imposing their fears on others, or worrying their families.

Just as support groups are important for those facing a serious, chronic and possibly life-threatening illness, so, it has now become clear, are they indispensable for complementary centres themselves. Unless they can all support each other, they will always be vulnerable. So what has happened to Bristol since the Chilvers report, and its attendant negative publicity, plus the entirely positive aspects of the formation of the Bristol Survey Support Group and the Patients and Supporters' Panel, which came into being after the success of the BSSG?

Here Bristol patient Jane Metcalfe, who was diagnosed with cervical cancer in 1989 and who now helps to integrate a holistic approach into the wider community, takes up the story.

Jane Metcalfe's story

When I was told, at the age of forty-one, that I had cancer of the cervix, I was not really surprised, as I had experienced a great deal of stress in the three years leading up to diagnosis. In fact, learning that I had cancer was, in some ways almost a relief because, although it was a terrible shock, at least it gave me the opportunity to take stock of my life and make a new start. At least, I now knew the worst.

I had trained as a singer and had spent most of my professional life in the highly competitive world of opera. People always imagine that being an opera singer is a glamorous job and of course it can be, but the pressures, the sense of elation at landing a plum role and the terrible feeling of rejection when you're not chosen, can lead to extreme highs and lows, which can be difficult to handle.

Nobody outside the opera world is aware just how much your life depends on the quality of your voice, and just how much intense work you have to put in to make sure your voice is always up to standard. As a singer, your body is your instrument, and it has to be kept in good condition. You carry your instrument around with you all the time, and this can make you highly histrionic – leading in some cases to the temperamental reputation that divas have. Also, unless you are one of the top few you may have to take jobs that you don't want, simply because you have to make a living.

I think my problems, which eventually led to my system breaking down and cancer taking hold, manifested in 1982, after my son was born. I was married to another singer, and we were having financial difficulties.

Throughout my twenties and early thirties, my career had gone wonderfully well. I spent four years with the D'Oyly Carte Opera Company, where I was principal mezzo-soprano. I also appeared with the

English National Opera, the Opera Factory in Zürich, and was involved in many other exciting ventures. The future seemed positive.

But after my son came along, it all seemed to collapse. As my husband and I were both struggling, I started to teach to pay the mortgage and didn't seem to have much energy to devote to my singing career. I had already had a breakdown in my twenties, which perhaps made me more vulnerable. At the time, I enjoyed teaching but, looking back, I think now that I built up a backlog of resentment, because I wasn't doing as much singing as I really wanted.

Added to that, our son was a non-sleeper, and I spent the first three years of his life in a constant state of exhaustion. My lack of energy and interest in pursuing my career, combined with the constant tiredness and the feeling I was operating at less than my best contributed, I believe, to the rapid breakdown of my marriage, and this led to more problems.

My then husband went back to Switzerland, his native country, and fought me for custody of our son. This led to a tug-of-love situation which resulted in ever more stress, but I bottled this up and stoically carried on coping, or trying to. At the same time as all this was happening, I was becoming increasingly disillusioned with the world of opera.

The problem with this world is that you have so much to live up to. Opera singers are so high profile, so fêted, so admired, that there is always a great deal of performance anxiety. Also, opera buffs are extremely critical people, finding fault with the merest flaw in your performance. It was as if the reality were not living up to the dream, and in the midst of all this, I seemed to lose touch with myself. Of course, as a performer, you are continually playing roles, which can stop you from facing up to who you really are.

I was trying to make a living, gain custody of my son, and also cope with the accusations of my ex-husband that I was a bad mother and not fit to look after a small child. I had little money, certainly not enough to fight a battle through international courts, and everything seemed hopeless.

I remember a terrible feeling of worthlessness, as if I had failed at everything. To make matters even worse, I encountered disapproval from other people for, as it seemed, abandoning my son. I felt I had failed as a mother.

All my life I had been looking for love. I suppose we are all doing this, but for me it was very intense, a greater or more urgent need than it may be for some others. At any rate, it led me into some very stressful and difficult relationships. At the back of my mind, I wanted somebody to look after me while I pursued my career. Unfortunately I always seemed to fall for the sort of man who wanted me to look after him, perceiving me, perhaps, as a strong woman. So things never worked out.

I was always looking for something outside myself, not feeling complete in myself and, with hindsight, that was why none of my relationships worked out. I had not yet learned to rely on my inner resources. During this period of financial hardship, while my marriage was floundering, I entered into another relationship, with an artist this time. He had come along as a breath of fresh air during the breakdown of my marriage.

By this time, I was in my late thirties, and all my dreams were fading. I had dreamed of being a famous opera singer at the same time as finding a man who would look after me and be endlessly supportive. Somewhere at the back of my mind there remained this fantasy of a very special man who would devote himself entirely to me so that I could abdicate responsibility for myself. I saw some of my friends marrying men who worked in the City and earned lots of money so that they could carry on singing, and just choose the roles they wanted and which suited them, without having a care in the world.

Probably it wasn't like that, but suddenly, everything seemed so unfair. I was getting ever more resentful that my life wasn't panning out as I thought it should. My relationships were in a mess. Looking back, I can see that I was very bitter because I couldn't do what I wished. For years, I had an image of myself as young, glamorous and successful, and here I was, feeling I was getting old without having achieved what I wanted.

I had set so much store by youth, and it was fast fading. I simply could not see myself as an old, or even a middle-aged person, only as a young one, and of course this added to the stress.

I had thought that I would only ever be regarded as an important person by my physical appearance and by the quality of my singing, and that if these went, I would be left with nothing. I began to feel truly hopeless, especially as my new relationship wasn't working out either, and I realised that, yet again, I had bought a fantasy. I thought that the end of my life had come, and this was another reason why I was not surprised to get cancer – and in an area which was at the very heart of my femaleness and femininity. I had become a deeply insecure woman.

In view of all this, it will probably not seem all that surprising that my health broke down. I had been experiencing very heavy bleeding between periods, which left me exhausted. It got so bad that I had to go and lie down in the afternoon. I already had had cervical smears, but they showed nothing.

Because I was still having so very much trouble with my periods, I went back to the doctor, but nothing seemed to be wrong. Then one smear I had showed some cell changes, and I was told to go back in six months' time.

I wasn't happy, though, and warning bells rang in my head. My parents had always believed in natural medicine, and at the same time as seeing my orthodox doctor, I was working with a naturopath. It was he who suggested I should have another smear and be seen by a specialist.

My own doctor had said that the smear came back clear. If I had taken any notice of him, I would have been dead by now: no question of it. But the specialist performed a colposcopy, and took a biopsy. We both knew something was seriously wrong, and the specialist said that he wanted me in hospital within a week for an operation for cervical cancer.

It turned out that the cancer was quite seriously advanced. I now consider myself lucky to have had surgery, because it undoubtedly saved my life. I had a hysterectomy, which was quite traumatic, but at least, I thought, I've had my family and I knew I did not want another child.

I was relieved to get rid of the bad periods, but glad to be able to keep my ovaries so that my body could continue to work naturally for as long as it would have done without the operation. Although it is very traumatic to lose a breast, in that it can be seen, it can seem as bad to lose your internal organs, and to have the knowledge that now there is nothing left of your secret womanhood.

I went to Bristol six weeks after my operation. I had heard of Bristol, of course, and had always been intrigued by its methods. This was before the Chilvers report came out, in 1989, and at a time when Bristol was on top of the world.

What happened to me there was a total revelation, but not necessarily in the way I had expected. As I took part in the various therapies, the counselling, the spiritual healing, the group discussions, I realised something very important for the first time ever: that I could ask for help from other people, that I no longer had to pretend that I could cope with everything alone, and that I was in total control.

My week at Bristol helped me to realise that I had a lot of problems to deal with, not only with my present situation, but with my past and my family. While I was there, I discussed a dream I once had of my father wrapped in bandages, and when I unwound the bandages there was nobody there. The interpretation of this was that my father was the invisible man who had never been there in my childhood. I then began a journey of understanding how my past experiences had affected my present way of being.

I realised that I could actually use my emotions and express them rather than bottle them up. I could be myself and did not always have to play a part – the part of the famous opera singer, the part of the mother, the part of the breadwinner, the part of the lover, the part of the wife. I came to understand that these were all roles I was playing, that any one could be taken away from me at any time, and indeed had – even the role of mother – but they were not the essential me, which was separate from all these. I became reawakened to a sense of the spiritual nature of myself, and the realisation that I was more than a body, more than presenting symptoms of cancer.

Going to Bristol also helped me to realise that I was not alone, that there were other people in the same position as me, and that we could all help each other. My time at Bristol enabled me to understand the utmost importance of self-help and support for cancer patients, to help them cope with a disease which is capricious, which can strike at anybody, and against which there are no guaranteed defences.

Nobody was suggesting at Bristol that we should abandon orthodox medicine. Conventional surgery had definitely saved my life, and I was more than grateful for it. At the same time, there was no set-up to help me cope with the emotional impact of getting cancer and the trauma of losing my internal organs at a time when I should still have been a fully functioning woman. There was nobody to help me understand the existential crisis that having cancer evoked. Bristol provided the environment which helped me towards a new way of living my life. With cancer, I began a journey of self-discovery.

My involvement with Bristol

So how did this lead to my becoming involved with the Bristol Centre?

When I came home from Bristol after my residential week, my mind was racing with ideas. I felt that what I had experienced there was so important, so valuable and so life-enhancing that somehow I had to pass it on to others. A few months later, my local consultant, a very open-minded man, told me that there was a conference in London called Cancer and the Mind, at which there would be speakers from all over the world. He suggested that I went.

It was a huge event, attracting about 400 delegates who were trying to understand what part, if any, the mind played in cancer. The conclusion was a resounding "maybe" – but the subject was being opened up, and seriously discussed.

Now for the past 2,000 years or so, physicians have debated the part that mental attitudes might play in cancer, but as yet there are still no firm conclusions. For me, though, it was exciting enough that all over the world there were people who were discussing the subject, and that among these were many orthodox cancer specialists.

I found the actual medical side of the conference daunting, not having much medical knowledge of my own, but the mental and emotional aspects made complete sense. It seemed as though scientists were beginning to take seriously the idea that the mind might play a far larger part in cancer than had been previously admitted, and I found it all very stimulating and thought-provoking.

It came to me in an absolute revelation that what cancer patients needed to support their orthodox care and the mental turmoil that the disease engendered, was a "Bristol" of their own. We all need a Bristol, I decided, a place where we can meet other cancer patients, discuss our treatments and problems in a group, and also take part in natural therapies such as massage, diet, spiritual healing and relaxation, to strengthen the immune system and help ourselves to become healed. At this stage, I was unaware of the rapidly growing self-help and support movement. It seems, as Jung suggested with his theory of the collective unconscious, that others were tapping into this idea, as I was doing.

So when I got back to Hastings, I made enquiries as to whether there were any Bristol-type centres in my area. The Bristol experience should not, I felt, be available only to those very few people who could get down to Bristol itself.

As there was nothing in my area, I felt the only thing to do was to start a Bristol-type centre of my own. To this end, I got together with my local consultant, and we decided to put on a conference. We invited all the big names in the orthodox and the complementary cancer worlds to come and speak, people such as Penny Brohn and Professor Karol Sikora.

The conference was a huge success. Although nothing like it had ever happened in Hastings before, we attracted nearly 300 people, many of whom were health care professionals and all of whom were fascinated at the ideas being put forward. I spoke to Penny and mentioned my idea for starting a Bristol-type centre in my own home town. She was very enthusiastic and the upshot was that my consultant and I decided to co-found a cancer help centre.

Of course we had no money and no premises, but none of this seemed to matter too much, and I set myself to fundraising. Karol Sikora, who was also my cancer consultant, agreed to become president of the proposed centre. I started a support group for cancer patients, and did a lot of publicity.

One of the fundraising events I organised was a big garden party. I will remember the date for ever: 3 September, 1990. Karol Sikora came to the party and said to me: "I think you'll find something has happened which may change the face of Bristol."

I had no idea what he was talking about at the time, and he wouldn't be drawn further. But on 6 September, Chilvers leaked out, with almost unrelievedly hostile publicity.

Overnight, all the interest in our proposed centre fell away to nothing. Nobody wanted such a centre any more and, to make matters worse, we were refused charitable status by the Charity Commission. We were turned down, unbelievably, on the evidence of an article in the *Daily Telegraph*, expressing grave doubts about Bristol's approach. We gained charitable status in the end, as we could not be turned down on the basis of a speculative view, but the centre as I had envisaged it was doomed. The Hastings Cancer Help Centre is, I am now glad to report, running a thriving support group.

I learned that the same thing had happened with complementary medicine: interest dwindled. Nobody now wanted to be associated with it publicly. It was as if it had never been. I could not at first understand how the findings of the report had attracted such vitriolic comments on Bristol, on complementary and holistic care generally, and on what had been widely acknowledged to be a healthy diet, even if it had never become universally popular.

As I read the newspaper reports and comments and listened to news items, I knew that something was deeply, deeply wrong, and that nobody could possibly be made worse by going to Bristol. Bristol could not do harm, under any circumstances. I had been there, and I knew.

It seemed to me that what I had to do was to pitch in and try to help undo the Chilvers damage. The report and its aftermath had taken power away from many cancer patients, and pulled the rug from under their feet. They had their support and help systems removed without any clear basis or evidence for this. The report threatened to kill off our own proposed cancer centre, the Bristol Cancer Centre and complementary therapies.

I felt I could not just stand by and let this happen. I arranged a forum where I asked some of the authors of the Chilvers report to speak, and also staff from the BCHC. It became clear that there had been a mistake. From then on, I became embroiled in investigating what the Chilvers report was really about, what accounted for the deep hostility to Bristol and, by implication, complementary cancer therapies generally.

From the moment the report hit the headlines, Bristol began to flounder. Most cancer patients who had visited and stayed at the Centre over the years, had elevated it as this big important Centre, and given it almost Godlike status. Many of us who had been to Bristol felt that it had changed our lives in fundamental and important ways. The Centre itself seemed like a rock, an ocean of calm and stability in the turmoil of cancer and cancer treatment, and here it was, the staff unable to cope themselves, flattened by one hostile survey which wasn't even accurate.

The carers, the nurturers, needed nurturing. I realised, as did the Bristol Survey Support Group later, that Bristol was simply not prepared for attack, that in common with so many complementary centres, they were isolated, vulnerable and, to some extent, in some ways, naive in the ways of the world.

They thought, as do so many people with a vision, that because what they were offering was good, because people demonstrably felt better, they could not possibly be doing anything wrong. The Bristol staff were not working for personal gain, kudos or status, but were quietly helping desperately ill and traumatised people back to mental, emotional and physical health.

I also felt that one of the reasons Bristol was so surprised by the attacks was the staff had always maintained that patients should continue with their orthodox treatment. There had never been any suggestion that the Bristol programme would supplant what orthodox oncologists were trying to do – but that it would, rather, help patients to deal with the emotional impact of a life-threatening disease. So it did not seem possible that those in the orthodox world could turn against Bristol as so many appeared to have done.

From the start, the focus of the staff at Bristol had been entirely concentrated on getting people better, in mind, body and spirit. Because of this, and because of lack of time and resources, they perhaps did not appreciate the importance, in our present scientific world, of systematic evaluation. They had never been able to undertake such a task themselves, and this was possibly one reason why they had been so keen to co-operate with the cancer charities on the survey.

Because I was an outsider, yet at the same time a cancer patient who had benefited immeasurably from going to Bristol, I felt I could see these things clearly. I decided to do a bit of networking myself, among former Bristol patients and support groups, to gauge the reaction.

Bristol remained so devastated by the attacks a year after the report that they said they were thinking of closing for a month to take stock. I was afraid that if they closed, they might never open again. A member of the Bristol staff asked me what other similar residential centres there were around the country, and I was amazed she didn't know. I was also astonished at how very isolated they seemed to be. It seemed to me that

Bristol had operated in a spirit of loving and giving, but had never realised that it must protect itself against possible enemies and give itself a firm base.

It became clear that Bristol had problems of its own, that it had undealt-with business to settle. While things were going well, the possibility of the Centre having its own internal difficulties never cropped up. Life was too successful, too comfortable. Chilvers provided the painful crisis which forced Bristol to look at itself, and see how it could keep going and remain relevant.

As happens so often with people on receiving a cancer diagnosis, Bristol's own fighting spirit was challenged as a result of Chilvers. Dr Mike Weir, who was at the time acting as a consultant to Bristol, asked me to research regional facilities, as he recognised that Bristol, in order to survive, had to forge stronger links with both the orthodox and the complementary cancer worlds.

It gradually became clear to me that scientists and orthodox cancer doctors, on the whole, had never liked or approved of Bristol, and were delighted to see the Centre rubbished. The reason for this is that the Centre held up a mirror to the orthodox worlds, and helped to bring about results which had been impossible with their expensive, high-tech treatments: that of enhanced quality of life. Their anger came from their sense of helplessness, that with all their training, all their expensive research and equipment, they couldn't do something that a simple centre, housed in a former convent, staffed by loving and kindly people, had been doing for years.

Bristol had succeeded in making the orthodox world feel very uncomfortable. But their reaction to Bristol was emotive and irrational.

For years, the Bristol Centre had enabled patients to look at and face difficult issues in their lives, and now it was having to do the same for itself. It was a time of immense pain and several times Bristol nearly went under. I felt that I was qualified to undertake the task of helping Bristol forge the necessary links in the wider world because, apart from being Bristol-minded, I had actually been a cancer patient and, because of my stage experience, was not afraid to speak in public.

Penny Brohn had been a wonderful spokeswoman in the past, but as she was no longer there, they needed somebody who had experienced a similar revelation to hers, that our stress and personal problems contribute to cancer. Apart from Penny, very few of the Bristol staff had ever been cancer patients themselves.

I had become aware that what gives people confidence is support groups, who in turn needed encouragement and support. Bristol retained me as a consultant for six months, during which time I was to go out into the community to see what kind of groups already existed, and what the attitude was towards Bristol following Chilvers. Also, I felt it was important to let people know that Bristol had survived.

It was also clear from my visits to regional centres that a growing number of people in the orthodox world were trying to understand the holistic approach, and to see how they could use it in their own work. The problem was that few were expressing public support for Bristol or its therapies.

In the end, I feel, the Chilvers report did not do Bristol lasting harm – it just enabled a change of direction and attitude to take place, and it was possibly the time anyway for a new look at what was on offer. In fact, the whole Chilvers episode highlighted the need for a new kind of evaluation of complementary therapies, which can be seen as the positive coming out of the seemingly negative.

I particularly felt it was important for people to be able to go to Bristol at an early stage of their cancer. In the past, patients had mainly gone when they were desperate, when they had been told by doctors that there was nothing further that could be done. If we could get this message out to more people, we would be able to attract the newly diagnosed, and at that stage harness complementary and orthodox techniques to provide the best possible care available. As I went round the regions, I heard so many people saying: if only I had known about this approach before, it would have saved me so much anguish.

Many patients I talked to on my tour of the regions told me they felt bitter and resentful because nobody had told them that there were valuable ways in which they could help themselves. If they could have discovered Bristol – or, at least, its approaches – early on in their cancer, a huge amount of fear and anxiety could have been relieved.

We have to understand that not everybody can actually go to Bristol for a variety of reasons. Nor can Bristol itself directly help every single cancer patient. Currently the Centre is consolidating integration of the holistic approach in hospital settings. In a pilot project which took the Centre's approach into hospitals, the Centre demonstrated what the possibilities were if a more total approach to cancer care was offered at an earlier stage in the disease. The response was overwhelmingly positive.

Much of Bristol's future lies, I believe, in education and the work in the regions is part of this educational process. The Centre continues to offer a very wide range of educational programmes for health care professionals and cancer carers as well as patients themselves. It has been found that patients will frequently do what their doctors approve of, so the Centre's courses are geared towards educating health care professionals in the holistic approach which may then encourage patients towards their own self-empowerment.

In fact, complementary therapies are being taken more seriously by hospitals, partly owing to patient demand. Mount Vernon in Middlesex, for instance, has its own purpose-built cancer support and information centre, which offers some "gentle" therapies and, in particular, counselling, often found to be of so much benefit.

Professor Karol Sikora's oncology department at the Hammersmith Hospital, London, offers complementary and supportive help, which developed from his own visit to Bristol in the eighties. He believes that the future of cancer care lies in an integrated approach.

At the time of writing there is no overall policy concerning the development of complementary therapies in NHS hospitals. It has tended to be a somewhat hit-and-miss affair, depending on the beliefs of the consultant in charge. Basically the demands of patients themselves will lead the way forward, so that a deeper care of the whole person will, one hopes, eventually be considered a perfectly natural way of dealing with disease.

I am often asked, in my travels, whether I will talk about breast cancer, cervical cancer, lung cancer and so on. My reply is that it doesn't really matter what kind of cancer you've got, as the emotional impact is the same. Patients with breast cancer, cervical cancer or whatever can discuss their treatments with each other, but Bristol's purpose is not to discuss the relative merits of different kinds of orthodox treatment.

So far as we're concerned, all cancer patients are the same in that they are facing a severe crisis in their lives, a crisis where their bodies have gone out of control and are rebelling against them. The place to discuss orthodox treatment is with orthodox specialists. Although Bristol has amassed an enormous amount of knowledge and information on cancer over the years, they are not experts in conventional treatments, and do not consider it their business to advise patients on these matters.

Bristol's job is mainly spiritual and supportive; to help people come to an understanding of cancer, which will enable them to regain the harmony they have lost, and of which loss cancer is a dramatic reminder.

Yes, "miracles" sometimes seemed to happen, but they can never be promised or guaranteed. What Bristol maintains is that through the severe crisis of an illness a new and more positive attitude can emerge, one which may enable us to see our cancer, as Lawrence LeShan has called it, as a turning point, rather than something unequivocally terrible.

PART TWO

THE BRISTOL THERAPIES

Introduction

This introduction to the therapies on offer at Bristol is meant to be just that – an introduction. Whole books have been written on all of these complementary therapies, and if you want to delve any deeper into them before deciding whether they might be for you, please refer to the Useful Addresses section at the back of the book.

Bristol cannot offer every single type of therapy, but the staff have put together the package which, after many years of seeing cancer patients, seems to be the most beneficial. You may find others which suit you, and there are many different ones, as you will discover if you join a patient-support group. Other members will have had experience of complementary therapies and can pass their thoughts and experiences on. Of course, what suits one person may not appeal to you, but we can't emphasise enough the importance of accessing the feel-good factor.

When the Bristol Cancer Help Centre first opened its doors to cancer patients, most of the people who went were desperately ill, had come to the end of the orthodox line and had been told there was nothing further that could be done. Now, cancer patients are encouraged to set their self-healing process in motion as soon after diagnosis as possible, so that conventional and complementary therapies can work in harmony and the quality of life can be optimised.

Bristol holds a variety of courses for patients with all types of cancer, and at all stages of the disease. For most people, a week, or even a day, spent at the Centre, is a revelation, leading to a magical realisation that a cancer diagnosis does not have to lead to permanent feelings of despair, hopelessness and constant fear. In fact, hundreds of people have realised that, in their own lives, their cancer has been a turning point leading to greater self-awareness, empowerment, positivity and assertiveness.

It is not uncommon for people to say, after the event, that their cancer was the best thing that ever happened to them. What they mean is that, but for such a severe crisis, this whole world of self-care, self-healing, self-nurturing and realisation that they are valuable, unique, special, worthy people might never have been opened up to them and they are grateful for the opportunity to take a close look at themselves and their lives. Cancer is, above all, a disease which often forces self-awareness on people, simply because it is so frightening and because there are no guaranteed cures or treatments.

In an ideal world, every cancer patient should have a "Bristol", a place or an opportunity to get to know themselves, to be able to dispel fear and anxiety, to take responsibility for themselves, at the same time as having whatever conventional treatment seems best for their particular tumour. At the moment, though, such places are not widely available, and we recognise that it is not possible for everybody to go to Bristol. So, in this second half of the book, we describe the therapies which are on offer at the Centre, and which have been found particularly helpful for cancer patients.

All are gentle, none is invasive, and all will help to harmonise mind, body and spirit to bring about the best possible environment and attitude for deep healing to take place. You do not of course have to have cancer to benefit from these therapies. They will bring about higher levels of health for everybody.

We realise that not everybody will take to everything that is described on the following pages. Patients coming to courses at Bristol are offered a taster, a sample, of the various therapies, so that they can decide for themselves which ones appeal to them.

Some people find they take enthusiastically to the diet, others discover that relaxation, meditation and visualisation work for them. Yet others find strength and solace in group work or in counselling. We cannot say that any of these will send tumours away so that they will never come back, or that they will enable the body to get back into such a glowing state of health that the cancer can never return.

Nobody, whether in the orthodox or alternative world, can make such a promise. We still have a very long way to go before anything can claim to be a definite cure for cancer.

When Bristol first opened its doors, it was almost impossible for cancer patients – or, indeed, anybody whether seriously ill or in good health – to put together a package of complementary therapies. The few that were on offer were haphazard, hard to find and were often extremely expensive. Now, at least to some extent, times have changed and many of these treatments have become widely available.

At the same time, a growing number of cancer hospitals recognise that gentle complementary therapies can help both with the emotional shock of a cancer diagnosis, and to aid the orthodox treatments which may be recommended. The educational work of the Centre is helping health care professionals to take on board the approaches which Bristol have pioneered, and it is hoped that this work will enable the self-empowering message to reach an ever wider audience.

One question which is often asked is: if I follow these therapies, the Bristol Diet and other holistic approaches, will these prevent me from getting cancer in the first place? Sadly, nobody can be absolutely certain of this. All we can say is that the risk of succumbing to any serious or life-threatening disease must be considerably lessened when the immune system is strong, when stress is not allowed to build up, and when resentment and hostility, or a perception of being a victim, are not present. It is becoming ever more apparent, through the new science of psycho-neuroimmunology (PNI), that many diseases are, above all, diseases of fear.

We die of fear more than of anything else. If a doctor tells a patient there is nothing more that can be done, the patient frequently gives up hope and dies. Whenever hope is taken away, the way is paved for disease to take hold. Hope is never abandoned at Bristol – because hope and excitement for the future is the most valuable healing tool that any seriously ill person can have. Nor does Bristol ever use the word "terminal".

Of course, none of us can do anything about our genetic inheritance or predisposition, and we may not be able to do much about our particular environment, either. We have to put hope, positivity, self-awareness, into a realistic context and understand that we cannot always control our own fate, our own health. But we can always make things better.

When the Centre first started, there was Pat Pilkington with her wide experience of spiritual healing and running a healing ministry, Alec Forbes, who had researched the dietary and bodily aspects of self-healing, and Penny Brohn, herself a cancer patient and also a practitioner of acupuncture. Together, these three people were able to devise a programme which would address in an interlinked way the mind, body and spirit. None of the therapies or treatments was invented by Bristol staff or doctors, but researched and put together for the first time in a specific programme for cancer patients. Penny Brohn, of course, had direct experience of alternative approaches to cancer from her long visit to Josef Issels' clinic, and was able to see what a dramatic difference the therapies there made to patients' attitudes. For the first time, cancer patients were not being treated as passive victims, but as thinking people who had something valuable to contribute to their own healing process.

In those days, all the ideas which Penny brought back from the Issels clinic seemed startlingly new – and for that reason could easily be dismissed as cranky. As Bristol expanded and became more confident, new therapies continued to be taken on board. There are now art therapy, music therapy, massage, shiatsu and circle dancing sessions for instance. But still the emphasis is on the holistic approach, the integration of all these aspects, to provide a wide-ranging healing programme.

Many cancer patients find that their orthodox treatments are uncomfortable, painful and frightening. By contrast, complementary therapies are gentle, working to lessen fear, stress and anxiety.

Complementary treatments will never *replace* conventional cancer care. What they do is enable you to look after and enjoy yourself while you are getting better. Never think of the Bristol therapies as medicine. They are, rather, wonderful healing tools which we all deserve, whatever our state of health or illness.

We have to learn to be kind to ourselves – and the programme of therapies which together make up the Bristol approach – show the way to do this. They encourage us to take an active part in our healing process, rather than just passively accepting invasive treatments.

Whether or not you decide to go to Bristol, whether or not you are a cancer patient, you can do nothing but benefit from the therapies described here, as all help to integrate and harmonise mind, body and spirit – however you may view the spirit.

5

Nutrition

The Bristol Diet, as it is widely known, has attracted more comments, criticism and controversy than any other single aspect of the Bristol programme. It has been called cranky, unproven, tasteless and pointless – usually by people who have no idea what it is all about.

The rationale of the Bristol Diet is that a food intake which is low in toxicity, which is easy to digest and which does not contain artificial ingredients, preservatives or stimulants, will provide the best internal environment for the body to maximise its own healing abilities.

The Centre has compiled a large nutritional database with relevant research and scientific studies into the relationship between health and diet drawn from all over the world, and which is updated as new evidence appears. In the past, the Centre had to go on gut reaction, common sense, logic and the experience of patients, plus a few research findings.

There is, at least, no evidence that a wholly vegan, organic diet based on grains, pulses, raw vegetables and fruit can *harm* you in any way, and plenty of indications that this kind of eating can aid not only the body, but the mind as well.

There is in the East an ancient belief that the kind of food you eat, and even the way in which it is cooked, can intimately affect thoughts, emotions and attitudes. Food which is over-preserved or artificial, and has had all the life taken out of it, is supposed to damp down thoughts and emotions; food which is over-spicy and overloaded with taste sensations can engender aggression and anger, whereas natural produce prepared with love and a calm, meditative attitude can clarify the mind and aid benevolence, love and tolerance.

There is a considerable body of research to show that a vegetarian intake reduces the risk of high blood pressure, heart disease, cancer, gynaecological problems, allergies, migraine and digestive disorders of all kinds. The reason for this, it seems, is that vegetable produce is kinder to the system, and is easier to digest.

When the body is compromised and highly toxic through cancer – and don't forget that many cancer treatments are themselves extremely toxic, particularly chemotherapy – the less work it has to do to digest and get rid of substances it is not designed to handle the better.

The Bristol Diet makes sense, even if we cannot point to hard evidence that it will shrink this or that tumour, or protect against succumbing to cancer in the first place.

The big problem with any diet is confusion. Nowadays, there are so many "healthy" diets promoted, and so many seem to contradict each other, that it can be hard to know what is best.

At Bristol, the approach is simple: it concentrates on vegan, organic, simply prepared dishes which do not contain salt or sugar. There is always a fresh salad, and fresh fruit. The Centre provides food which is as near to its source as possible, and the only element of animal produce on offer is cows' milk for those patients who simply cannot bear, or cannot take, soya milk in their hot drinks. Fish and chicken can be obtained for those patients with cancers affecting the digestive system. There is no coffee or alcohol, and the food is all gentle rather than stimulating.

Bristol does not claim to have all the dietary answers, and its own diet has been modified over the years to take in new evidence, new findings. But basically, there seems to be no need to move away from the natural, all-vegetarian diet initially introduced by the Centre's first doctor, Alec Forbes.

The Bristol Diet has never been intended as a penance or punishment, but as a reintroduction to healthy eating which has been lost in our age of food technology and artificial colours and flavours. However, we must admit that for a large majority of patients, it has felt like a penance, because it does not have the "quick fix" element of instant snacks, caffeine-containing drinks and highly stimulating tastes. Even nowadays, many years after the Centre opened, it is noticeable that most cancer patients are not eating at all healthily, and a healthy diet is rarely mentioned by doctors and orthodox cancer specialists.

Previous books on the Bristol Diet have paid a lot of attention to theories about whether protein, fats and certain types of carbohydrate can affect cancer one way or the other. Dr Josef Issels maintained that cancer was, above all, a metabolic disorder, an indication of a highly toxic system. His view was that, in order to be well, the whole body had to be treated, and this meant a rigid adherence to certain dietary principles. Dr Issels' view was that you had to change the *milieu* so that it became impossible for the cancer to grow in your body.

The regime practised at Dr Issels' clinic in those days was adapted for use at Bristol. Don't forget, though, that the Issels treatment was supposed to be a complete alternative to conventional cancer care – and this has never been the case at Bristol. Nevertheless, many of his views and theories made complete sense to the Bristol pioneers.

The Ringberg Klinik's approach was aimed at raising the body's own defences against cancer, and at the heart of this was detoxification therapy. Josef Issels, and Max Gerson in America, favoured coffee enemas on the basis that coffee absorbed through the rectum causes the gall bladder to flush out bile and toxins, and reactivates the liver.

Dr Gerson's dietary therapies are so very complex that as well as being a full-time job for you, the patient, their preparation – fruit and vegetable juices every hour – needs a full-time helper as well. But again, Dr Gerson's clinic provides a complete, not complementary, treatment for the cancer patients.

The nutritional regime adopted at Bristol, after investigation of the Issels and the Gerson approaches, consists of: no animal protein, no stimulants in the form of tea, coffee or alcohol; no artificial flavourings, preservatives or colourings; no salt, no sugar, and as much raw food as possible. The diet is also low in fat.

In her book, Penny Brohn writes feelingly of the attitude of most of Issels' patients to the Diet: one of deprivation and of extreme guilt when a minor dietary rule was infringed. At the Klinik, Penny noticed that often she was the only person who ate more than a token helping of the food set out buffet-fashion: loads of raw vegetables and salad, muesli for breakfast and a kind of porridge, with honey or butter being provided with the utmost unwillingness by the kitchen staff. Nobody, she says, apart from herself, liked or looked forward to the food, and she only liked it because she was already used to eating this way.

For most patients, even in these days of widespread promotion of high-fibre, low-fat, fresh foods, the diet comes as rather a shock, and as something to get used to, although some people are delighted to discover the clean taste of unadulterated food.

It is not always appreciated that it can be difficult to change your diet, mainly because habits have set in and, as with all habits, the more they are repeated, the more firmly established they become. The way we eat becomes a ritual and also a kind of addiction. We "have" to have our morning cup of tea, our mid-morning coffee, our chocolate snack, our Coke, or whatever. When these are not available, we feel deprived, and indeed we are deprived, because the body gets used to all addictive substances.

Food is also a highly emotive subject. For while most cancer patients will not have experienced spiritual healing, art therapy or music therapy, it is an absolute certainty that all will have experienced eating, and many do not like their prejudices to be challenged, nor to be made aware that there might be something they can do to improve or modify their eating habits.

Kate was diagnosed with bowel cancer in 1990. Even before attending Bristol as a patient she had embarked on the diet as outlined by Dr Alec Forbes in his book. She said: "I felt the benefits almost immediately. I had been living on takeaways before I was diagnosed, and never gave much thought to the quality of food that I ate. Certainly, fresh vegetables were never a priority.

Now, even though I have had a section of my bowel removed, I have no problems coping with the high degree of raw foods recommended on the diet.

Occasionally, I do slip back into old ways of eating – and I notice the deterioration in my health almost immediately. So now I try to eat basically vegan food at home to maintain my sense of well-being.

I don't like the word 'strict' being used in relation to the diet, as this sounds punitive, and I have never thought of the Bristol Diet as any form of punishment. I love the kind of food I eat now, and feel much cleaner for it. Sometimes, if I feel I need it, I go on a completely raw food diet for a few days, and this seems to clean me out even more.

I must say that my partner supports me in the diet, and this is important, as if you have somebody at home trying to sabotage or make fun of your attempts at healthy eating, it becomes much more difficult. But then, he has grown to enjoy the food as much as I do. For us, it has become a way of life, and neither of us could contemplate returning to our old habits.

Jane Metcalfe tells of her experience of the Bristol Diet:

I was brought up a vegetarian, but had strayed at varying times in my life. After touring the States in the seventies, I suddenly found I could no longer tolerate the large red steaks that seemed to be the mainstay of most hotel restaurants. Overnight, I ceased eating meat. However, I continued to include fish in my diet, as well as eating more salads and fresh vegetables. This state of affairs lasted until the mid eighties, when I lapsed into the "bacon-butties-and-coffee" syndrome as my personal life began to cause me distress. I was also the kind of person who binged on chocolate, which resulted in feelings of self-dislike and guilt.

When I began to feel physically ill, just before the cancer was diagnosed, I consulted a naturopathic doctor, who put me on a dietary regime similar to the Bristol Diet. In addition, I was allowed only water to drink, which I found excruciatingly difficult. However, apart from losing excess weight, I began to feel full of energy and lighter in spirit than I had done for years. In fact, I now believe that this cleansing of my body helped me to cope both mentally and physically with the cancer treatment. Putting good, clean food into my body made me feel more in control, and I remember friends bringing me exotic fruits to eat in hospital instead of chocolates. Giving my body the best possible chance of recovery by eating the best possible foods made complete sense to me. I suppose I was a bit of a "born-again veggie" for a time, but I hope I never forced my ideas on those around me.

By the time I went to Bristol I was thoroughly used to their way of eating, and found the food instantly delicious. Yes, I did miss the coffee and tea to begin with but, when tempted to stray, the desire to stay well was great enough to prevent me yielding to temptation. I suppose I saw myself initially as a kind of laboratory experiment, and to this end I became my own guinea pig as I tried different ways of making basically bland foods palatable.

I enjoyed making new and exotic dishes, delicately and gently flavoured with spices, and friends who came to dinner were always appreciative of this way of eating. I now find that sugar and salt mask the individuality of different food tastes, and that cuttting them out allows the palate to experience the subtleties of original taste.

During the nine-month period in which I stayed faithful to the Bristol Diet, I gave myself the occasional treat such as fish and chips. I felt I needed this reward from time to time to acknowledge my hard work, but it did not turn into a craving. It is essential not to feel deprived on the diet and, particularly for cancer patients, not to feel guilty if you can't always stick to it.

We are all human, and therefore fallible. One very wise therapist I know uses the expression: "Anybody with a belly button is entitled to ten per cent error." This is a good reminder not to beat ourselves up if we consider we have failed. As time went by, I added organic wine to my treats list, and had the occasional cup of coffee.

It was not always easy to find a good variety of organic vegetables at first, so I tended to mix and match, eating organic whenever possible. Most of all I learned to approach eating with a sense of enjoyment. It is most essential to eat in a relaxed manner, enjoying your food. If we regard it as a penance, no matter how good the food is for us, we may lose its positive properties by our negative attitude.

My son, who was seven when I contracted cancer, now has his favourite veggie dishes which he "commissions" in the holidays. Yes, he eats meat with his father, but accepts my way of eating as perfectly normal, too. He loves shepherdess pie and vegetarian spaghetti.

I am often asked how I stick to the diet, and the answer is that whenever I feel I have gone into toxic overload by eating too many fast foods, having a glass of wine too many or an overdose of caffeine, I revert to my Bristol regime for a while to cleanse the system. I seem to have developed an inner sense that lets me know – usually by lowered energy levels and disturbed sleeping patterns – when I am on the slippery slope to unwise eating. As a rule, at home I eat in the Bristol way, but when out I eat as wisely as my particular environment will allow. I don't, though, allow myself to get into a state if I have to rough it now and again.

For me, diet is part of a whole approach to health and it does not dominate my life. I believe it is as important to clear the emotional and mental toxins as it is to clear the bodily ones. Indeed, to me, they seem inseparable. A desire to eat well can be born out of a clear mental state and vice versa.

There are many different so-called anti-cancer diets and they can be a minefield for those embarking on a nutritional approach to health. Therefore, Bristol has, over the years, simplified its diet in order to make it less daunting to those used to the average Western diet. Bristol recognises that it can be difficult to change the habits of a lifetime, and cancer patients are encouraged to try and change gradually, if the diet is not immediately appealing. Of course, there are cancer patients who may wish to attempt a much stricter regime than Bristol suggests, and this is fine as well.

There are a number of cancer patients who remain faithful to Dr Alec

Forbes' original Bristol Diet, which is much less flexible than the one offered today, yet the overriding principles remain the same. As with all of its therapies, Bristol recognises the right of the individual to choose what appeals to him or her the most.

Now, let's take a closer look at the tenets of the Bristol Diet: low protein, low fat, no dairy produce, no salt, no sugar, natural food, raw food, as they apply to cancer patients.

Low protein

Vegetarians are often asked how they can be sure they are getting enough protein. Well, one thing is certain in the Western world, and that is that nobody is going short of protein. The "great British breakfast" was instituted only at the beginning of this century, when it was seen as important to build the man of the family up to do a hard day's manual work. Now that many people work in sedentary occupations, and ever fewer do hard manual labour, it is simply not important to eat as much protein.

The fact is, we as humans don't need animal products to keep the system strong, healthy and energetic. There is no evidence that deficiency diseases result from lack of meat intake. In fact, it's more likely that a high-protein diet will itself lead to illness, to the "diseases of civilisation" such as cancer, heart disease and diabetes.

Until recently, the main evidence for a low-protein diet lessening the risk of cancer, comes from religious groups such as the Seventh Day Adventists, who are strictly vegetarian and also take no stimulants such as tea and coffee. Results of recent research into the health consequences of a vegetarian diet published in the *British Medical Journal* also support this view.[1] It also seems that some types of tumour feed on protein, and the more you eat, the more they take – at the expense of the body.

Don't imagine just because you may not be eating fish, meat or poultry, that getting enough protein will be at all difficult. Grains, pulses, wholemeal bread, rice, nuts – especially almonds – all provide good quality protein, and a satisfying protein-filled meal would be baked beans on toast. Baked potatoes and hummus with salad also provide a balanced meal. This kind of meal is not at all difficult to prepare, and in fact you can find it ready-made at most supermarkets if you are unable to cook for yourself.

The intensive farming methods by which much modern meat and fish comes to us is based on lack of concern for the animal or its proper breeding cycle. At Bristol, where the emphasis is on gentle healing, the attitude is taken that it cannot be good for an already immune-compromised system to eat animals which have been artificially fed and fattened, and reared by methods which involve cruelty.

The authors of this book firmly believe that we simply don't need animal protein and are in fact far better off without it – our digestive systems have far more in common with vegetarian animals than carnivores.

[1] *BMJ* 1994; 308: 'Risk of Death from Cancer and Ischaemic Heart Disease in Meat & Non-Meat Eaters'.

Low fat

Low-fat diets have become increasingly popular since the early nineties, and were given a great boost by Rosemary Conley's controversial *Hip and Thigh Diet* books. Conley's diets are based on an anti-gallstone diet, which of course excludes all fat.

There is, as yet, little specific evidence that a high-fat diet predisposes to cancer, except that a high-fat diet is likely to be one rich in all the substances which the body finds hard to digest, and which may clog the system.

Avoiding dairy produce and meat means that the diet is automatically low in fat, and correspondingly low in calories. At Bristol, no animal fats are ever used to cook food, and instead, cold-pressed vegetable fats and oils are used.

Dairy produce is avoided at Bristol because it clogs up the system, causes excess mucus and is in any case unnatural to a grown-up body. No animal apart from humans feeds on milk products after being weaned – that is, on a natural diet. In addition, milk products contain growth hormones, which in some cases may encourage the growth of tumours.

Natural food

By this, we mean organic, unrefined, unprocessed food. A few years ago, it was difficult to obtain organic foodstuffs, but now most supermarkets have them. The reason Bristol recommends organically produced foods is that many vegetables and fruits grown in non-organic soils do not have their full complement of minerals and vitamins. So you are more probably eating depleted foods, even if they are raw, and eaten soon after the day of purchase.

Many artificial foods contain substances which may be carcinogenic. At any rate, the body's systems are not designed to handle artificial colours and flavours, and attempting to digest and cope with them puts one more strain on the body.

Bristol recommends organically grown produce where possible. Yes, it is more expensive than the other sort, but if you're not eating other expensive items, such as meat, fish and dairy produce, you will probably find that your weekly food bill is still cheaper than before.

Raw food

This is more controversial, as one of the more famous anti-cancer diets is macrobiotic, where most of the food is cooked. In her book *Gentle Giants*, Penny Brohn describes how some seriously ill cancer patients at the Issels clinic found the raw food difficult to digest.

It's something you can get used to – but it's perhaps not the kind of food to suit everybody. The main advantage of raw food is that it retains most of its "goodness" – the vitamins and minerals which can easily be leached out during the cooking process. Bristol also likes the idea of "living" foods rather than dead ones, which is another argument for a high-raw intake.

Bristol used to be quite strict about raw food, but now accepts that many cancer patients, particularly if they are suffering from mouth, throat, stomach or bowel cancers, may find a lot of raw food hard to digest. In cases where raw food cannot be tolerated, it is advisable to steam vegetables lightly.

Unless your cancer directly affects the digestive system, though, there is no reason why you would not be able to eat at least fifty per cent of your food raw. Start off with organically produced apples and carrots, and proceed from there.

The question of salt

Salt, once considered essential for taste and flavour, is now going very much out of fashion anyway. You will notice that old people use far more salt than young ones and, as a nation, we seem to be losing our enthusiasm for it.

It used to be thought that salt played a definite part in the rise of cardiovascular disease, but this is not now so certain. In fact, very few theories about food have become cast-iron and salt is subject to many differences of opinion. The main reason for avoiding salt is that it contains a lot of sodium – in fact, the chemical name for salt is sodium chloride – and this tends to reduce levels of potassium, which all cells need for optimum function.

Very many nutritionists and also unorthodox cancer doctors, in particular the late Dr Max Gerson, believe that at least some types of cancer are associated with a low-potassium diet. At the Gerson clinic, patients are put on a high-potassium diet, in the belief that most chronic disease in the body is intimately associated with loss of this mineral from body cells. Some cancer authorities believe that the high incidence of stomach cancer in Japan is connected with the high levels of salt in the diet.

A diet which is high in raw food and low in fat will automatically be one which is low in salt. Most preserved foods, at least the savoury variety, contain a great deal of salt or monosodium glutamate, and by avoiding these you will automatically be avoiding excess salt intake.

Of course, we do need some salt, but natural and raw foods by themselves contain all you need. If you have acquired a taste for salt – and as with most food tastes, this is acquired rather than innate – try taking less. You will most likely discover that you start to prefer the more natural, more subtle tastes of the food itself.

The sugar question

Perhaps you hardly need telling that sugar is bad for you – after all, you have been told this, most likely, since childhood. It's certainly bad for your teeth. Sugar is a highly addictive substance containing mainly, as we all know, empty calories.

Sugar is never used at Bristol, and honey only sparingly. Sweet tooth? We can recommend Green and Black's organic chocolate, which is seventy per cent chocolate, and very low in sugar. It will satisfy your sweet-tooth craving, and also a craving for chocolate, if you have one, without doing your system much harm. But do avoid highly sugared puddings, sweets and desserts, also highly sugared fizzy drinks.

Stimulants

By this, we don't mean street drugs, but the ordinary drugs which we take several times a day such as tea and coffee. Caffeine has been associated with both cancer and heart disease in animals and although there is no absolute proof that it contributes to cancer, it certainly blocks the action of prostaglandins, and causes stimulation of the nervous system.

Caffeine stimulates the adrenals, and gives us a hyped-up sensation. It also dilates blood vessels, and encourages carcinogenic substances known as nitrosamines to form in the stomach.

Try to wean yourself off tea and coffee if you find you are drinking more than three cups of either or both a day. There are very many herbal teas and coffee substitutes on the market, and you may have to shop around until you find one that suits you. If you simply can't do without your cup that cheers, try decaffeinated coffee made by the water method, a non-chemical way of getting the caffeine out of the coffee. You can also get decaffeinated tea, and a good one low in tannin is Luaka, now available at most supermarkets.

If you feel you simply can't give up your tea and coffee, try to drink them early in the day when they do less harm, and when your system has more time to cope with them. If your cancer is affecting your liver, you would do better to try to avoid tea and coffee altogether, as they contribute to the toxic overload on this vital organ.

Because these beverages are so highly addictive – coffee is the most popular beverage in the whole world – they are among the most difficult things to give up entirely. Also, tea and coffee are intimately woven into our social and working lives. They seem harmless, but don't forget that they are not natural substances by the time they come to us, but highly processed and artificial.

If you drink lots of water during the day, and get into the habit of doing this, you will gradually find that your addiction to tea and coffee lessens. If you are an addict – and you won't really know until you try to give them up – you may find you experience quite bad withdrawal symptoms.

Some health experts believe that giving up tea and coffee, for hardened addicts, can be as bad as withdrawing from heroin. But usually, if you can stand it for a week, you will have overcome your addiction.

Alcohol should definitely be avoided by anybody with liver cancer, as the liver has to work hard to detoxify the effects of alcohol in the body. If possible, try to do without alcohol. If this is not possible – and don't forget that alcoholic drinks contain a lot of refined sugar, and reduces the amount of vitamins B6 and C in the body – then try to stick to wine from organically grown grapes.

Over the years at Bristol, it has been found that patients have widely varying attitudes to the diet. Some take to it straightaway, and never return to their old eating habits. The majority take some benefit, but do not stick to it strictly once they get back home.

It is all too easy to slip back into old eating habits, as the kind of foods we don't recommend are the most seductive, easily eaten, strong-tasting kinds which appear to be instantly satisfying, such as a Big Mac.

But don't ever forget the powerful psychological impact of being able to change your diet to a healthier one. Whenever you are able to take charge in this way, self-confidence increases and, with it, self-esteem and greater assertiveness. Once you have been able to take control of eating in this way, you are ready to take control in other areas of your life.

Vitamin and mineral supplements

Do we need them on a healthy diet or not? A few years ago, most orthodox nutritionists maintained that, on a healthy balanced diet, we simply did not need extra supplements. Now, they are changing their tune, and recommending at least vitamin C and E for the maintenance of healthy systems, as these vitamins help to scavenge out free radicals, best explained as oxygen particles which rust up the body systems in the same way as rust on a car.

During active cancer, high dosages of supplements as a boost to the diet are recommended as it is impossible to obtain sufficient levels of necessary vitamins and minerals from food alone to fight the cancer. It is not possible to detail which dosage, as this depends on the type of cancer, and how compromised the immune system is. Recommended supplements may also depend on certain kinds of orthodox cancer treatment, such as chemotherapy.

As everybody's supplement needs will be different, there can be no hard and fast guidelines. There are nutritional experts at Bristol who can give advice, but in general, cancer patients would benefit from Vitamin C and E supplements, vitamin B complex, zinc, potassium, selenium and beta-carotene.

All these items are essential for proper cell functioning, and are easily lost through orthodox cancer treatments. The Centre provides a leaflet on request with details of these vitamins and minerals, and a publication *Cancer and Nutrition: the positive scientific evidence*, incorporating recent research findings supporting the Centre's nutritional approach.

Another popular supplement is the preparation known as Iscador, or mistletoe. The rationale for this is that as mistletoe is a parasite preying on its host plant, it will act in the same way on cancer cells, which are also parasites. Iscador forms part of the homoeopathic treatment of cancer, and many Bristol patients have gone on to use it as prescribed by a homeopathic doctor. Iscador can be prescribed by your own GP. Iscador is mainly injected, and patients who would like to use it will usually have to learn to inject it themselves. The therapy has been extensively studied in Europe, and there is evidence for its efficacy. The Centre recommends Iscador, but does not actually administer it, as it forms part of medical treatment for cancer, which the Centre does not see as part of its job.

Here are some typical Bristol-style recipes to get you going towards a healthier eating pattern. All the dishes are easy to cook and prepare, and are not expensive.

6

Bristol Recipes

An Introduction by Wanda Nowak
Chief Bristol Cook from 1990

In devising these recipes, my main motivation has been enjoyment of healthy, natural ingredients. It seems to me that changing our eating habits should not be an ordeal but a time to experiment and discover new flavours and tastes.

I feel it's best to take dietary changes gradually. You may like to change your breakfast first, before making more fundamental changes with other meals. It is also important to be able to treat yourself, even if your idea of a treat is chocolate fudge cake or a fry-up – so long as this is done in moderation.

Cooking and eating healthy food should not be a stressful business, and don't worry if you find it difficult or impossible to give things up immediately. And always remember: replace, rather than leave out. Perhaps our motto at Bristol should be: slowly but surely!

THE RECIPES

Note: all serve four, except whether otherwise stated

Rice Porridge

5 oz wholegrain rice (short or long grain)

1 litre soya milk

1. Place the above in a slow cooker overnight ready for breakfast, *or*
2. Cook as traditional rice pudding in the oven on a low heat (gas mark 3) for 1½ hours, or until the rice is soft. Serve with a little date syrup or soaked prunes or apricots.

Hummus

2 cups (14 oz) chickpeas
2–3 lemons
4 tbsp tahini
4 fl oz olive oil

3–4 cloves garlic, crushed

To garnish: parsley, lemon slices, paprika

1. Soak chickpeas overnight, rinse and drain. Boil in fresh water until soft,
   – about 1½ hours. Drain, saving liquid, or use tinned chickpeas.
2. Put chickpeas into blender with one cup of cooking liquid, add juice of
   one lemon, the tahini, the olive oil and some of the garlic. Blend well.
   Taste and adjust the seasoning, adding more lemon and garlic as you
   like.
3. Serve in a pâté dish with slices of lemon, sprigs of parsley and a
   sprinkling of paprika.
   Serve with wholemeal bread and salad.

Carrot and Lentil Soup

6 oz red lentils, dry weight
1 onion, diced
4 cloves garlic, finely chopped
2 tbsp olive oil
4 carrots, chopped

1–2 tbsp tamari
3 cups water
1 tsp freshly ground black pepper
juice ½ lemon

1. Cook lentils in the water until soft – about half an hour.
2. Sauté onions and garlic in the oil for 10 minutes.
3. When soft add rest of ingredients except lentils.
4. Simmer until carrots are soft, then add cooked lentils and blend.
5. Add lemon juice at end for zing and sprinkle with a little chopped
   parsley, if liked, to serve.

Vinaigrette

½ pint cider vinegar
¼ pint cold-pressed extra-
    virgin olive oil
¼ pint apple concentrate

1 tsp mustard seeds soaked
    in apple juice until soft
pinch oregano (or any herb)
freshly ground black pepper

1. Blend the above in a liquidiser or stir briskly by hand. Serve with salads.

Spaghetti Vegetariana

4 oz green lentils, dry weight
1 onion, finely diced
1 tbsp garlic oil (or olive oil)
1 green pepper, finely diced
4 oz mushrooms, sliced
1 courgette, finely diced
1 tin organic tomatoes, or
    1 lb fresh tomatoes, blended
3 tsp tomato purée

1 tsp mixed herbs
1 tsp celery seeds
½ tsp mixed spice
1 pinch freshly ground black pepper
1 tsp tamari (soy sauce)
1 tsp apple juice concentrate
3 oz wholewheat spaghetti,
    dry weight, per person

1. Cook lentils in plenty of water until soft – around half an hour.
2. Sweat onion in garlic oil until soft.
3. Add pepper, mushrooms and courgette and cook for a few minutes,
   stirring continually.
4. Add tomatoes, purée, pepper, herbs and spices.

5. Add cooked lentils, tamari and apple concentrate. Simmer gently for 10 minutes.
6. Bring large pan of water to boil. Cook spaghetti in water for 12 minutes or so until cooked. Serve with the sauce.

Tofu Nuggets

1 x 8 oz or 10 oz block tofu
½ pint tamari
½ pint apple juice
1 tbsp ginger juice (root ginger grated then squeezed by hand)

1 tbsp rice flour
pinch black pepper
garlic oil – or garlic cloves marinated in olive oil

1. Cut tofu into 2in cubes.
2. Marinate in tamari and apple juice for 40 minutes in the oven at gas mark 6 with ginger juice.
3. Drain tofu, keeping marinade in jar in the fridge.
4. Toss tofu in seasoned rice flour.
5. Brush baking sheet with garlic oil and bake tofu with a dab of garlic oil for 20 minutes at gas mark 7.

Can be served sprinkled with lemon juice and as an accompaniment to stir-fried veg and brown rice.

Parsnip and Cashew Bake

1½ lb parsnips, chopped
1 lb onions, finely chopped
1 tbsp olive oil
6 oz cashews
6 oz mushrooms, sliced

1 tbsp garlic oil
pinch black pepper
1 heaped tsp mixed herbs
1 tbsp tamari

1. Steam or simmer parsnips until soft.
2. Sauté onion in olive oil.
3. Bake cashews on shallow tray until golden brown (8 mins at gas mark 8).
4. Sauté mushrooms in garlic oil until just soft – 5 minutes.
5. When parsnips are soft, mash them well and add the pepper, herbs, tamari, onions and cashews.
6. In ovenproof dish, put layer of parsnip mixture, then mushrooms, then rest of parsnip mixture. Bake in medium oven for about 40 minutes or until golden on top.

Fruit Crumble

2 bananas	*Topping*
2 apples	4 oz oats
1 tbsp raisins	2 oz sunflower seeds
1 tsp cinnamon	1 oz brazils
1 tsp mixed spice	1 oz cashews
¼ pint apple juice	1 tbsp olive oil
	1 tbsp date syrup or apple
	concentrate

1. Chop fruit and place in ovenproof dish with raisins, cinnamon, mixed spice and apple juice.
2. Grind up oats, seeds and nuts and mix in oil and syrup. Stir or hand mix until you get a crumble consistency, adding more oil if necessary.
3. Spoon on to fruit, press down and bake at gas mark 6 for about 40 minutes.

Mousse

1 heaped tbsp agar agar flakes	1 pint soya milk
⅓ pint water	⅓ pint fruit concentrate

1. Put agar agar flakes and water into small saucepan. Bring to boil and gently simmer, stirring constantly until flakes have dissolved.
2. Put soya milk and fruit concentrate in liquidiser, add agar and blend well.
3. Pour into sundae glasses and chill in fridge until set.

Soya Cream

1 pint soya milk	1 heaped tbsp leftover rice
2 tbsp apple concentrate	porridge, or ½ block of tofu.
juice and zest of 1 lemon	
dash vanilla essence	

Blend the above in liquidiser until smooth. Chill and serve.

Note: All the dry ingredients, the oils and herbs, can be obtained from most health food shops. Increasingly, supermarkets are also stocking "health" foods.

7

Visualisation

Most people who have any knowledge at all of complementary cancer therapies will have heard of visualisation, the self-healing technique developed in the late seventies by American cancer specialists Carl and Stephanie Simonton.

This involved seeing the cancer cells in concrete terms and then imagining them leaving your body. The most famous image conjured up by the Simontons was that of visualising the white cells of the body as sharks attacking the cancerous cells, which were visualised, for some reason, as a cauliflower.

Once hailed as a powerful tool in self-help against cancer, visualisation has not been shown to be the dramatic cure once imagined. However, this does not mean that it has no place; indeed, it can be a very effective means of bringing about what you would like to happen, whether or not you are a cancer patient.

Put very simply, visualisation is the ability to form an image in your mind and keep it there, until the desired change is brought about. The image can be negative or positive, but its strength will determine what you are able to bring into being. Visualisation by itself may not be enough to get rid of all the cancer cells in your body, but it will certainly encourage you to send them packing. If you can strongly visualise your body being completely clear of cancerous cells and tumours, your body may well receive, hear and understand the message.

At the very least, the techniques of visualisation will aid your orthodox treatment and give you a positive attitude towards your own healing. It enables you to feel that you are putting something in, being active rather than simply the nervous, frightened recipient of treatment.

The technique is by no means new, and has been used since ancient times by psychics, clairvoyants, healers and shamans of all kinds and in all societies, who understood that before anything can happen, it must be clearly visualised. It works like this: if you want to be rich, for instance, you don't just sit there and hope that one day your ship will come in or you will win the pools. You see yourself as already a rich person, and keep that image constantly before you, unchanging and unwavering. In time, if the visualisation is strong enough, you may well become rich.

Conversely, if you see yourself as poor and powerless, this is what you will become. If you see yourself as young and vibrant, you will stay young and vibrant. If you see yourself as ill and frail, that is what you will become.

If you see yourself as an angry person you will become angry. However you see yourself, this is what other people pick up and feed back to you.

When it comes to cancer, it's important to find an image which suits you, and which you can easily keep in your mind. It is always helpful to see the cancer cells as weaker and more chaotic than whatever you visualise to send them away. At Bristol, patients are asked to provide their own images, but always it must be that of a powerful force and an already weak opposition. If you see the cancer cells as being strong and powerful in their own right, then visualisation won't work for you – except, perhaps, that you may even increase their power.

Heather, who attended as a patient, says:

> Visualisation is sometimes seen as a difficult technique, something only those with a trained visual sense or a strong imagination can do. In fact, visualising is a very natural activity, and something we do all the time. It is simply that in healing it is done for a purpose and in a more deliberate way.

Frances, another Bristol patient, had a lumpectomy for breast cancer in 1985. She was already involved in complementary medicine and had trained to be a reflexologist, so the Bristol approach was not entirely new to her. However, she was not clear at first what were the differences between meditation, relaxation and visualisation. She says:

> Going to Bristol sorted things out in my mind. I understood the difference and found visualisation particularly helpful. I devised my own imagery that made me feel in control. As I live by the sea, I imagined my cancer was like mouldy bread, and I threw it out to the seagulls. Then I took it one step further and actually threw out my stale bread to real seagulls! It felt very powerful and really made me feel better, working on my cancer being eaten up for real! Each person needs to find an image that works for them.

In the early days of using visualisation as a complementary cancer therapy, patients conjured up all kinds of exotic images. The problem was, if they were unfamiliar, it was difficult to keep these in the forefront of the mind. Also, for those who are not in the habit of imagining or visualising things, this can prove hard work indeed, and may not be very productive.

The point is that the image, whatever it may be, must be constantly there, and you must never forget about it. Don't forget that there are no limits to your imagination, and no limits to what you can do with your cancer in your mind.

Jane Metcalfe has found visualisation an extremely powerful anti-cancer tool, and describes her experience of using this technique.

> My visualisation worked by my being able to see myself going up in a transparent bubble and ejecting my cancer into space. To make it safe

for the environment, I then turned the tumour into a star. The ability to do this enabled me to lessen my great fear of the cancer. I saw the tumour being safely removed, with no harm to anybody, especially myself.

But that imaginative image wasn't the only extent of my visualisation. I also saw my operation going without any hitches, and visualised myself being well and whole afterwards. I visualised the wound healing, and these were of course very simple images, not requiring a great imaginative leap.

People who come to Bristol often say they've got no imagination. Also, some of them confess to feeling silly when they try to conjure up unusual images, partly because they believe that they have to come up with something startling.

But it's not necessary at all. Visualisation can be very simple indeed, and all it need mean is that you think of yourself as a whole, healed, well person. I actually don't think it's a good idea to think of the cancer too much at all, as that way you keep your attention focused on it, and what you think about grows in your mind.

Also, if your tumour has gone, and you are clear of the cancer, it's not very helpful to keep thinking of it in cancer terms.

After my operation, I visualised a beautiful red rose in place of my uterus, which had now gone.

Penny Brohn said in her book *The Bristol Programme* that when she wants to get rid of her cancer, she makes a mental picture of all her cancer cells piled up in front of her on a plate in the form of ice-cubes. She then takes them and puts them in the full glare of the sun in a beautiful garden and watches them melt away.

Penny advises ending any visualisation session with the cancer completely overcome and melting away. Some patients find this hard to do, she added, because they know their cancer has not gone away, and that it is still palpable and painful. But at Bristol, patients are always encouraged to end up with a mental picture in their minds of being completely free from disease.

Visualisation sessions at Bristol focus on patients seeing themselves as perfect human beings, spiritually, mentally and physically. Unless we can do this, we risk limiting what we can achieve, and it's as if we are saying to ourselves: you can be a little bit better, but not completely better. We have to allow ourselves to impose no limitations whatever in our minds – and to keep bearing in mind that we deserve the best, that we deserve to be free from worry, stress, tension and fear – all of which crowd in to stop us from getting better.

Although many patients who come to Bristol describe very unusual images to send away the cancer, the best one by far is simply to imagine yourself well. Penny Brohn suggests remembering yourself as completely healthy in the past as, if you've got cancer and it is very serious, it may be difficult to visualise yourself being well in the future. Then, by keeping in mind a strong image of yourself when you were well, you can start projecting into the future, and hold on to this picture of yourself as vibrant, healthy and fully healed.

Unfortunately, some cancer patients have such low self-esteem and self-confidence that they cannot, dare not, imagine themselves as well and healthy.

At Bristol such patients are given specific help and constant reminders that they are special, unique, put on earth to sing their own individual song. Meditation, relaxation and proper breathing, which will be discussed in the next chapter, all help with successful visualisation.

Penny Brohn suggests this image for cancer patients trying to use visualisation techiques on their own:

First of all, picture your body healing itself. You don't have to think of any weird images for this, just imagine that it is slowly, gradually, getting better. As you do this, keep thinking of your white cells seeking out the malignant ones and overcoming them. Now try to imagine that your white cells, the ones that are designed to do this work, are beautiful, clean, white goats, benign creatures which are quick on their feet, agile, fast-moving and sure-footed.

These goats are moving throughout your body, eating up the unwanted rubbish and leaving the way clear. They will eat up nettles, they will use their horns to tear into tangles of weeds and they can chew up anything, even old hats and shoes. Once the goats have eaten up all your cancer cells, they are no longer harmful, in just the same way that nettles can't harm you once the goats have eaten them.

You can either imagine the goats at work in your body, or that your body is a meadow or orchard. When the tumour has gone, the goats can continue grazing safely and harming nobody.

A visualisation techinique that works for many patients is to set goals for the future. If you are determined to live long enough for some important event in the future, such as your son's graduation, or the arrival of a new baby in the family, then it's amazing how likely it is that you will live to see this cherished event.

Once you have taken on board the idea of visualisation, and are able to think up images which render the cancerous cells harmless and inactivated, you can start to use visualisation in other areas of your life. As you start to see yourself well and healed and whole, so you can start to view those around you in the same way.

If you are going for a job interview, for instance, you can visualise the interview going well, see yourself getting on with the interviewer, and imagine them shaking your hand and picturing your pleasure at receiving a letter of acceptance. If you visualise all this before going for the interview, you are much more likely to get the job than if you see it all going badly, and being interviewed by people who don't like you and who denigrate your skills.

Similarly, if you are taking an important exam or a driving test, visualise yourself doing well, being confident, remembering everything that is relevant and that you will give of your best. Such visualisation doesn't guarantee, of course, that you will get top marks in the exam or pass your driving test – you have to put in adequate preparation as well – but it makes it more likely. Also the power of visualisation is such that if you see yourself as having passed the exam or test, this makes you more inclined to do your homework beforehand.

The same with a job interview – once you can visualise it going well, you are more liable to prepare yourself properly for it.

The power of visualisation is that it enables you, gradually, to get rid of negative thoughts, of stress, anger, tension and anxiety, both concerning yourself and others. Everything proceeds from thought, and as thoughts can be negative or positive, so they will affect our actions. Even something as simple as making a cup of tea requires thought. You think: I'll make a cup of tea, and then you make one.

Visualisation works well with affirmations, which is just a way of saying that if we repeat what we want to bring about in the right way, our chances of bringing it about greatly increase. Simple affirmations which often work well with cancer patients include: I am attracting health into my life: every day, in every way, I am getting better; I am seeing myself ever more as a whole, complete person.

At the same time, we have to be careful that what we are saying, we really want. The mind has several levels, and what we want consciously may be quite different from what we want unconsciously. Unless you want to be well at a deep level as well as the superficial level, visualisation and affirmations won't work. They have to be the conscious expression of your deepest-seated desires.

For instance, we, the authors of this book, are imagining that every single cancer patient wants to be well and healed. But we know that this is not always the case. All cancer specialists are aware that some people, unconsciously, realise they are getting more out of being a cancer patient than they would be if they were well.

For instance, when you are a cancer patient – or, indeed, suffering from any serious illness – you are looked after, you are fussed over, people treat you as an invalid, and you may be excused all kinds of adult responsibilities such as looking after other people, or holding down a job. Instead of your looking after others, they now look after you. Also, you are having lots of treatment which, although it may be painful and debilitating, is also expensive and time-consuming. You are using up a lot of resources. You have specialists, doctors and nurses running around after you, important people whose only job is to try and make you better. Also, you don't just have any old illness, you have *cancer*, the most important disease of modern times, one for which there is no guaranteed cure, and which frightens everybody. Before your cancer you may have been a nobody, but now you are important. You are ill, you count, you have to be treated as a special person.

Of course, most people with cancer are not like this – but some cancer patients are, as indeed, are a proportion of all chronically ill people. The point about visualisation, meditation and relaxation techniques is that if this is your subconscious attitude, it may explain why you are finding it difficult to visualise yourself as a healthy person.

Some people also want to die – and for them, all the visualisation in the world about living long enough for an important event, will not make any difference. Cancer has been called the socially acceptable means of suicide, and for some people this is undoubtedly the case.

We are assuming that people who go to Bristol, and those who are reading this book, sincerely do want to get well. For you, visualisation will work if you decide now to incorporate it into your life. You can do it for yourself without any expensive equipment, lessons or courses.

The best way to start visualisation, or to make it an integral part of your life, is to sit down and think seriously and calmly about all the things you would like in your life. Assume for the moment that there are no limits on what you can achieve.

Now, think for a moment whether the things you really want are at all possible. You may now never be a prima donna, but have you always wanted to sing? If not, why not consider taking singing lessons? At the very least, your singing will be better than it was before, and you will lose your self-consciousness about it.

We can always enact change in our lives if we visualise it strongly enough, and then see how it can be brought about. It is important to bear in mind that we cannot change anybody else's behaviour or attitudes – only our own. But if we behave more benevolently to those who irritate or annoy us, we will encourage them to behave better anyway.

Whatever you would like to change, see it as if it has already happened. Visualisation works best when we are in a relaxed, calm state of mind – and in the next chapter we will discuss ways of breathing and relaxing so that a mentally and physically calm state is achieved.

Breathing and relaxation are very important aspects of the Bristol approach, as it is only when we are quiet and in a meditative frame of mind that we can halt the hustle and bustle of our minds and create the conditions which can bring about powerful, positive changes in our lives.

8

Breathing and Relaxation

Emphasis on proper breathing and relaxation are among the most important aspects of the Bristol programme. Most of us, whether we are well or ill, tend to breathe too shallowly, and rarely remember to take deep breaths. Although as infants we start off by breathing properly and naturally, as we grow up, fear, tension and anxiety tend to make us take too little air in when we breathe.

We all know what it's like to breathe quickly with fear or excitement – and there is nothing wrong with that. Shallow breathing helps us to face fear and danger when there is a need to stay and fight or to run away. But we also need to calm down – and the best way of inducing calmness into the body is to breathe deeply and rhythmically, in an unafraid way.

Unfortunately, cancer patients tend to be afraid and nervous all the time, because they know that they have a dangerous and capricious illness, liable to return at any time. Also, the treatments and consultations induce fear, worry and panic. The result is that, very often, cancer patients particularly breathe in a panicky way – and then get into the habit of doing this all the time.

The result is ever more fear, panic and anxiety. When we are chronically nervous, exhausted or fearful we tend to hyperventilate, and this can make us hysterical. If you don't believe us, just try breathing fast and shallowly, as if some great danger was approaching. See how hyped up your systems become, and how this very type of breathing, even when there is no actual danger, sets up a sensation of panic.

Now, by contrast, try sitting in a comfortable chair, or lie down on a bed. Practise breathing very deeply and slowly. As you do so, you will be aware of how tension and anxiety are floating out of the system with every breath you take. Within a very short time, you feel calm and relaxed. You will also find that it becomes possible to think clearly as you breathe deeply.

When we pant and gasp, we can only react, we can't reflect. And the longer the body stays on red alert, and adrenaline is pumped into the system, the longer the panicky feeling lasts.

It has now been shown – and this will be explained in greater detail in the section on spiritual healing – that deep healing occurs when the body and mind are in a calm state. This calmness allows systems to regenerate, and the body to repair itself. As cancer is, above all, a dramatic indication of body systems and cells breaking down and running riot, it makes sense to do whatever you can to induce calmness and peace into your life.

If you are trying to come to terms with a serious diagnosis of cancer, you may imagine that there's not much you can do to alter your situation. But you can always bring calm and peace into little corners of your life by learning and practising deep breathing and relaxation.

At residents' weeks at Bristol, there are breathing and relaxation sessions every day, more than once a day, and it is always surprising how difficult many people find it to relax. We may imagine that relaxing is the most natural thing in the world – but there's more to it than sinking into an armchair and watching the television.

In fact, television is extremely unrelaxing as the images which constantly flitter across the screen work to maintain us in the hyped-up state. Also, we often have very strong reactions to TV programmes. We may laugh or cry or get angry, or otherwise express strong emotions – all counterproductive to effective relaxation.

We may also talk of a "relaxing" drink in the pub, or a "relaxing" evening with friends. In fact, the only way you can really learn to relax is in a special relaxation group, or by yourself. For so many of us these days, relaxation and deep breathing have to be learned and consciously practised, simply because we have got so out of the habit of being kind to ourselves in this way.

When we learn to breathe slowly and deeply, this alters our very consciousness, and enables the whole system, body and mind, to have a better quality of thoughts. In tranquillity, we can reflect, plan, decide – none of which we can do when we are hyped up.

The trouble is, most of us think we know how to breathe – or at least, we feel it comes so naturally that it doesn't have to be learned. But breathing exercises form a very important part of the Bristol programme, because the staff have learned that it's essential to learn how to breathe slowly and deeply and to be able to relax before any of the other positive changes in attitude or emotions can be brought about. Proper breathing is particularly important for cancer patients as cancer cells hate oxygen, and the more oxygen we can get into the body, the less likely malignant cells are to thrive and proliferate. Breathing and relaxation go intimately together, and are part of the same exercise. You can't breathe deeply unless you are relaxed, and you can't relax unless you can learn to breathe deeply.

Never imagine that because relaxation and breathing sound so ordinary, that they are unimportant. In fact, the more seriously ill we are, and the greater the fear and shock which is induced by the illness, the more essential it becomes to learn how to relax properly.

Jane Metcalfe writes:

What I've found is that most of us, including myself, are not naturally very good at relaxing, and cancer patients can find it particularly hard. The point about breathing and relaxation is that practising these consciously gives the body a chance to let go, and to calm down.

Because a diagnosis of cancer is so frightening, most patients are on continuous red alert, the well-known fight or flight syndrome which puts us in a state of suspended animation, waiting for an event which may never happen.

When cancer is diagnosed, we are in a state of fear. We fear for our present but particularly for our future – we worry that we may never have one, that the endless vista which only a few weeks ago stretched out before us may now be prematurely curtailed, before we have done any of the things we wanted to. Also, the thought of the treatments is frightening. We are terrified of surgery, terrified of being mutilated, and most cancer patients have heard stories about the nausea, pain and problems connected with chemotherapy. Most cancer patients see themselves being cut about, spending time in hospital, never being able to work again, being unable to look after their families. The future, which formerly may have seemed a pleasant prospect, becomes a place of terror. We project our fears into the future, whether or not these have any basis. The great majority of cancer patients cannot envisage the future with any kind of calmness or serenity at all.

For this reason, proper breathing and relaxation should be practised as soon as possible after diagnosis. You are in a state of total shock and can easily go into lock mode, where everything is frozen. Unless you take conscious steps to relieve your anxiety, you can get locked into this state permanently – and make yourself even more ill than you were before.

It's essential for all cancer patients to be able to alleviate the physical effects of fear. When we are in a chronic state of anxiety, we don't allow ourselves to let the energy flow. Deep breathing enables anxiety to flood out of the system. Whenever you are worried about your treatment, or whether the cancer has spread, you should practise deep breathing exercises to release this anxiety.

Bristol therapist Barbara Siddall puts a lot of emphasis on attention to deep breathing, coupled with conscious relaxation. She explains:

> Breath is our most vital force. We cannot exist for more than a few minutes without it. Water is our next vital need, and then food, but these are much less urgent than breathing. Breathing has many functions. These are that: breath feeds us, breath cleanses us; breath gives us energy and oxygenates our tissues. Breath enlivens our mind and thinking. Speaking needs breath to bring meaning. Breath teaches us about ourselves and others. Breath warms us. Breath is the life force and, as such, connects us with the universe.

Barbara points out that proper breathing, which is deep, slow breathing which goes right down to the diaphragm, forms the most important part of any yoga exercise. Proper breathing is a necessary practice to change consciousness and to bring about a meditative frame of mind – the consciousness where creativity takes place.

As babies, says Barbara, we naturally breathe correctly: from the abdomen, the rib cage, the back and the upper chest. But as we get older and experience fear, nervousness, tension, we forget this and start to breathe shallowly. In particular, we hang on to our breath when we are holding on to our feelings, and not letting them go. When we can release and free our breath, we can release and free ourselves.

As life speeds up, says Barbara, and becomes a competitive race, we start to breathe only in the upper chest, and the breath becomes fast, as breathing space is limited. Faster breath creates unease, and makes us feel constantly hyped up. The problem is that this kind of shallow breathing becomes a habit, so that in the end we imagine that it *is* proper breathing – if indeed we think about it at all, which most of us don't.

Penny Brohn believes that deep breathing, although important for everybody, has a special significance for cancer patients. One of the things she learned at the Issels clinic, she says, is that cancer cells thrive when starved of oxygen. Because of this, Josef Issels had developed two specific therapies to oxygenate the body. One of these involved injecting huge syringes filled with ozone into big muscles.

Issels' other method involved extracting some of the patients' own blood, oxygenating it and then putting it back. Penny experienced this treatment with terror, as she felt sure she would die from a stroke as she watched the now bubbly blood being reinjected into her veins.

Issels' views about cancer and oxygen remain controversial and are certainly not shared by all cancer experts. Some oncologists believe that it is actually impossible to get any quantity of oxygen into cancer cells, as the blood supplies to tumours are scanty and inadequate. They maintain that in order to get enough oxygen to the tumours to make any difference, oxygen would have to be pumped into the cells at a pressure which would be impossible for the body to take.

Whatever the truth – and bear in mind, that in spite of huge amounts of research, nobody knows exactly how cancer cells grow, develop and multiply – it seems common sense that deep breathing, coupled with relaxation techniques, must have a good effect on both the body and the mind.

Even if oxygen has little direct effect on cancer cells, the art of deep breathing is so ancient, and it is so well known that certain types of breathing can induce altered consciousness, that we believe it can have nothing but a positive effect.

At the very least, the ability to breathe deeply significantly reduces anxiety and tension.

The method of deep breathing taught at Bristol is very simple and can be easily practised at home. It should be practised every time you feel particularly fearful and anxiety-ridden.

Lie down in a comfortable position where you can be undisturbed. A good position to get into is the Alexander Technique one where you lie down on your back on the floor with your head supported by books until the whole of your spine touches the floor. Draw your knees up, and have your hands by your side. This position brings you back into symmetry and allows stress and tension to flow out of the body. People who practise the Alexander Technique often get into this position at the end of a hard or taxing day, to allow anxiety to flood out of the system.

It works best if you can lie still like this for fifteen minutes, allowing the breath to become slower and deeper. As the breaths become deeper, a feeling of calm takes over.

If you like, you can put on some relaxing music, such as whale songs, wave sounds or other gentle sounds. Experiment to see whether you prefer total quiet, or gentle music.

After you have brought your body into a state of harmony, bring your attention specifically to your breathing and concentrate on it. Do this for as long as it takes for your breathing to slow down, and for a slight pause to develop between the in-breath and the out-breath.

Put your hands over your abdomen, fingers touching loosely above the navel. Feel your fingers moving up and slightly apart as you breathe.

Now move your hands upwards and apart and place them at the side of your body, on your rib cage. You will feel the fingers being gently pushed outwards as your lungs expand. Do this for a few minutes.

This exercise can be repeated at any time of the day, and don't forget that deep breathing can be practised standing up. Relaxation is easier when lying down of course, but any time you feel your shoulders hunching, and that you are going into a fear mode, remember the deep breathing exercises.

If you find it impossible to practise deep breathing on your own, or don't imagine that you will remember to do it, you can join a yoga class which concentrates on breathing. Over the past few years, studies have shown that yogic breathing can alleviate a number of illnesses, such as asthma, diabetes and stress-related disorders.

At a yoga class, you will be taught how to breathe deeply, how to hold the breath, and how to bring the energy up from the base of the spine to the top of the head through breathing.

At one time, yogic breathing had a somewhat hippy image, but now it is being incorporated into many hospital treatments. The importance of deep breathing has been advocated for very many years by cardiologist Dr Peter Nixon, who believes that shallow breathing is associated with many negative emotions, with heightened arousal, with the inability to sleep and relax, and with chronic fear.

Chronic hyperventilation, he believes, causes the "effort syndrome" where we never feel really comfortable or at peace. Shallow breathing also alters the oxygen and carbon dioxide balance of the body, and means that our body cells are never able to get their full complement. When we breathe shallowly, or hyperventilate, we can become hysterical, bad-tempered, angry and over-aroused on a permanent basis, never giving ourselves the chance to become well and restore the body to a healthy state.

At Bristol, relaxation is taught in a group setting which can be much easier than trying to do it all by yourself. There are now many relaxation classes available for those who find it very hard to relax – and the experience of Bristol therapists is that cancer patients, above all, do find it hard to let go, to be positive, to be peaceful – and anybody who is experiencing difficulty with deep breathing or with relaxation, might find it useful to join a class.

One method of relaxation which works well for many people is autogenic training, which has been called "Western meditation". The meaning of the word "autogenic" is that you are enabled to bring something normally unconscious, such as breathing, into conscious awareness. Through autogenic training, you are taught to relax each part of the body in turn, by imagining it to be warm and heavy.

As you concentrate your thoughts on each limb in turn, you will find that they do indeed become warm and heavy and supremely relaxed. Although there are a number of books available on autogenic training, it is best to learn it in a class, or a one-to-one setting, as it can be frightening to do it on your own. Many people find that all kinds of unwelcome thoughts come to the surface, and a lot of pent-up emotion can be shed. This needs a safe setting.

At Bristol, people often become very emotional and start to cry, or to bring deep emotions to the surface that they may have buried for years. It helps if these can be discussed, or at least, allowed to dissipate and die down in a setting where everybody will be able to sympathise.

Some cancer patients find that the Alexander Technique is extremely helpful. This was developed over 100 years ago by an Australian actor, and is basically a method of unlearning bad breathing and postural habits. When you have got into bad habits over the years, you are probably not aware of them, and they may need to be unlearned with the help of an expert. Although primarily a body therapy, the Alexander Technique also often enables long-buried emotions to come to the surface, and to conscious awareness.

All of us, and cancer patients in particular, have buried painful and difficult emotions, and one reason for shallow breathing, for the "hurry syndrome" that pervades our lives, is the worry about activating these memories and emotions, for fear they will trouble us again. While we anaesthetise ourselves with hurry, while we remain workaholics, always rushing about here and there, or keep ourselves so busy that we never stop to listen to that still, small voice inside, we can imagine we are sending painful thoughts and problems away. But we never do. Unless we can allow deep emotions and worries to come to the surface they remain in the system like a virus. And although the virus can remain inactive when we are well, as soon as defences are down, it can start to become active again.

Coping with such a severe crisis as cancer gives us a chance to examine these buried emotions and difficulties, and to allow them to float away, troubling us no more.

It is only when such emotions are brought to the surface that they can be dispelled harmlessly, and allow deep healing to take place. It is impossible to be properly healed while negative emotions and thoughts are jumbling around in your mind. And while the initial memories and thoughts may be painful, once you have let yourself go through with them and acknowledged them, they need never bother you again. Once you have faced your demons, you can see them for the phantoms and chimeras they are.

Deep breathing allows us to start taking charge of our lives, to know who we are and to make a determined start to get well again.

As breathing is so essential to life, it makes sense to learn to breathe properly so that all body systems can operate at their maximum. This is of course important for everybody, but in particular for cancer patients whose immune systems and metabolism are so very compromised.

At Bristol, there is the belief that deep breathing should be taught as a matter of course to every cancer patient, as it is now well known that the fear experienced at diagnosis can, if not addressed, turn into terror which may develop into actual mental illness. The first thing any newly diagnosed cancer patient must learn to do, and the most important, is to incorporate specific techniques for alleviating fear and anxiety, so that they do not embed themselves permanently into the system.

We are not claiming that deep breathing will send away the tumour, or that it can prevent all anxiety.

What we can say with confidence is that it will bring about a more positive attitude to your life, and put you in charge rather than imagining you are a helpless victim of circumstances beyond your control.

9

Hands-on Therapies: Massage and Shiatsu

Massage

Massage has had a long hard struggle to make itself respectable as a complementary healing therapy. For too long, it has been associated with seedy parlours. It appears that this image has not entirely vanished, in spite of strenuous efforts of serious massage practitioners over the past few years.

Many of the cancer patients who come to residents' weeks at Bristol are extremely nervous of the massage sessions and are frightened of undressing completely in front of a stranger. This fear affects both men and women, possibly because, as adults, we are not used to being naked, except when being examined by a doctor, or with a lover.

Also, perhaps even more importantly, few of us as adults have experienced a loving touch which is not sexual, or has no seductive or manipulative overtones. So the idea of lying naked on a table while a masseur, usually a perfect stranger, goes all over your body using scented oils can be rather worrying. Often, as well, a bit of ego comes out: we would like to impress the person who is going to do the massage, with a beautiful, honed, toned, slim, tanned, perfect body. Nothing else will do.

The fact is, all professional therapeutic masseurs are used to working with every type of body and they are not there to admire or to sneer at your flab, your weight or your general appearance, but to seek out and smooth out tight, knotted muscles and tension so that you can feel relaxed and at ease, and certainly better for the massage than you were before.

Until the early eighties, massage, at least in the UK, was simply considered a pleasant indulgence. Then, largely thanks to the efforts of one woman, masseuse and beauty therapist Clare Maxwell-Hudson, it began to be incorporated into complementary therapies. One of the first doctors to use massage was Peter Nixon, a heart specialist at the Charing Cross Hospital. He realised that, in addition to their orthodox treatment, patients could also greatly benefit from a loving touch.

He invited Clare and her team to come into the hospital to offer massage to heart patients. Some of them were enthusiastic, while others were worried that they might have to take off all their clothes. So many heart patients were so unused to being touched, Clare and her team realised, that sometimes the most that could be done was to massage their hands. But even this became a method of healing, of enabling seriously ill people to start feeling whole again.

Medical and scientific research on massage has now shown that it can be a powerfully relaxing tool and, as such, can help deep healing to take place. Massage is now taught on nurses' post-graduate courses, and forms part of their training. It is also widely available for AIDS and cancer patients, in hospitals and at hospices. Very many elderly patients are now benefiting from gentle massage.

Cancer patients often fear massage more than others, because they may have had mutilating or serious operations. One resident at Bristol, commenting on the massage, said: "It's not very nice to expose yourself when you've got a bit missing." This patient had had a mastectomy, and had limited her life to the extent that she refused to go swimming or get herself into any situation where people might notice she was wearing a prosthesis rather than having a natural breast.

The thought of massage often brings home to breast cancer patients that, although prostheses can look very convincing when you are dressed, when you are naked there is nothing you can do to hide your operation. Although breasts are not normally exposed during massage – and you are kept covered up with towels all the time – the idea that underneath the towel there is a mastectomy scar can be enough to put many patients off the idea of a gentle massage. At Bristol, residents are given an opportunity to try it if they want to – but it is not compulsory.

The point about body massage is that it gives you a chance to integrate your body, to come to terms with and love it all. After a massage, you feel as if every part of your body is loved – and this is very important for cancer patients, who may have scars from their operations. It is also very nice to feel expert hands easing out the accumulated tension and stress from shoulders, neck and possibly buttocks.

Allowing yourself to receive a massage means that you are giving yourself up to pleasure and enjoyment. But if, as a cancer patient, you are interested in the idea of massage, it's a good idea to find out beforehand whether your masseur is used to massaging cancer patients, as it is important to know what to do around the site of the tumour. Professional masseurs will not massage around tumours and they may avoid scars, depending on their extent and how long ago the operation occurred.

Nowadays, most masseurs learn about tumours and how to avoid them during their training. Gentle touch is most important for pleasure, and it's also important for cancer patients, as for other seriously ill people, to realise that they can be touched, that they are not untouchable or unlovable.

Often, when we are very ill, we avoid other people's touch in case we contaminate them. Giving yourself up to massage can allow you to love yourself again, to understand that your body, even if racked with cancer, is not horrible, or unlovable, but can still respond to touch. Massage enables you to feel good about your body again – even if you have been through horrendous surgery and radiotherapy.

If you can feel good about your body once more, self-confidence is powerfully increased. Sometimes, we have to feel that we deserve massage, that we deserve somebody taking this sort of time and trouble with us.

Liz Hodgkinson talked to many who received therapeutic massage at Bristol. While at Bristol, Liz decided to sample the massage given by Andy, who has been a professional masseur for many years and also runs a training school in the town. Like most male masseurs, Andy is a gentle kind of man, somebody who believes wholeheartedly in the healing power of touch. He is aware, though, that cancer patients are often nervous about having a massage.

Andy massages with appropriate aromatherapy oils – a pleasing experience in itself – and is particularly good at getting out the tensions from the shoulders and neck. At times, patients experience something approaching pain as he unknots a specially tight muscle, but Liz's hour with him was the most relaxing of any she spent on her week at Bristol.

It's always better both for the patient and for the masseur if the patient can be naked, but no professional masseur will ever insist on this. If cancer patients feel happier wearing underwear, then this is fine. The patient is never exposed, but always covered up completely with a towel or cloth. As each part is massaged in turn, this is uncovered while the rest remains under wraps.

Most masseurs avoid overtly sexual areas, for both men and women, but some female masseuses may massage lightly over the breasts of their female clients, if this seems right. This can feel very nice, as sometimes one is powerfully reminded of sexual areas when the masseur is so careful to avoid them.

Massaging the breasts allows you to integrate them into the rest of the body, rather than thinking of them as something separate. Breast cancer patients – who make up the majority of visitors to Bristol – can start to feel horrible about their breasts, and a loving touch in such a sensitive area can allow them to feel better about them, or, if they have had a unilateral mastectomy, to feel better about the one that is left.

Above all, masseurs accept your body. Nowadays, all professional therapists will have massaged every type of body, including ones which are very old, crippled, or have had bits amputated. Massage is definitely not just for those who have young and healthy bodies. In fact, the more ill you are, the more you risk becoming alienated from your body, and the more therapeutic gentle massage becomes.

Don't forget, though, that the client is in charge of the session, and you can always discuss beforehand what kind of massage you want, and what might suit you better.

Cancer patients who attend residents' weeks at Bristol are reminded throughout the week that we live very much in our heads these days, and forget that we have bodies. A diagnosis of cancer, of course, is a powerful reminder that we do have bodies, bodies that can go horribly wrong and let us down. A gentle body therapy such as hands-on massage on naked flesh can put us back in touch with our bodies, and allow us to become one with them, to remind ourselves that mind, body and spirit are interrelated.

Cancer patients often come to hate their bodies for going so out of control. Having gentle massage can enable you to start loving your body again, to take loving care of this physical instrument of yours. Bodies, as well as minds, respond to being loved and touched, and we should all be aware that there is a loving touch which is not in the least bit sexual.

One male patient who was at Bristol while Liz was there was very nervous of having a massage. He was nearly seventy, and had never had one before. But he bravely decided to go ahead, and found it a wonderful experience. His body no longer felt so horrible, such a traitor to him.

Patients who are interested in massage may well find that it forms part of the complementary treatment available at their local hospital. Hammersmith Hospital, which has a well set up complementary care team, certainly offers massage, and it is gradually coming in at the more enlightened cancer hospitals.

Patients can also make enquiries of the Macmillan nurse or other cancer counsellor as to whether massage is available. Ideally you should go to somebody who is used to dealing with cancer patients, as this is not the same as sports massage, or physiotherapy. Otherwise, it's best to go on personal recommendation, if you can. Most towns now have complementary and natural health clinics where massage is offered. You can make enquiries here, and see whether the form of massage might suit you.

It is not a good idea to reply "cold" to an ad in the paper. Most local papers are now full of advertisements for masseurs and other natural therapists, but booking up people you don't know can be a great risk, especially if they will be coming to your home.

But don't rule out massage as not being for you if you have been very ill, or have had extensive surgery. Once you get used to it, its benefits can be enormous.

Shiatsu

Shiatsu, which comes from Japan, is another hands-on therapy practised at Bristol which is particularly helpful and therapeutic for cancer patients.

It is basically finger pressure, which is applied to various parts of the skin, on what are known as pressure points. The areas which are touched by the shiatsu practitioner are those where vital energy is strongest. Shiatsu is similar to acupuncture in that the practitioner follows meridian paths, except that no needles are used. The idea is that as these points are touched, energy which has previously been blocked starts to flow naturally. Then better health results.

In the East, shiatsu has been used for centuries, but it is fairly new to the West, and very new to cancer patients. One of the reasons that cancer patients often prefer shiatsu massage is that it is done through clothes.

Clients are asked to wear loose fitting, lightweight clothing preferably made from natural fibres. This means there is no sensation of the patient's skin, which means the therapist does not react to the skin being cold, warm, dry or oily. Instead, the deeper energies flowing throughout the body are accessed.

Shiatsu is not just a surface treatment. It realigns and balances and works on the acupuncture meridians of the body. It works by putting people back in touch with their breathing, and helping them to release and let go of pent-up stress and anxiety. The technique works to restore peace and calm throughout the body, and is particularly suitable for cancer patients because if one area of the body is painful or has a tumour, then the same energies can be accessed through another part of the body.

As with all complementary therapies, especially those where you are touched, the attitude of the therapist is important. She, or he, should be calm, responsive, non-judgmental and work with a combination of skill and intuition. Intuition as a quality should be cultivated by all complementary therapists, as they should be picking up from the client what the client most needs. This is one dramatic way in which complementary therapies differ from orthodox medicine.

Unlike ordinary massage, shiatsu is not always completely painless. Sometimes, quite acute pain will be felt in some of the pressure points. According to practitioners, this indicates blocked energy, known as *ki*. Sometimes, more than one shiatsu session will be required before all the blocked energy is released. Shiatsu is becoming extremely popular and is supposed to be especially good for bad circulation, reduction of muscle pain and fatigue. Enthusiasts claim that it can also treat high blood pressure, migraine, arthritis, diabetes, rheumatism and insomnia.

Ideally, if you are having shiatsu, this should be used in connection with a good diet and relaxation, proper breathing and meditation. As with most complementary therapies, shiatsu works best on a body which is calm and relaxed.

At Bristol, traditional shiatsu has been adapted by the therapist, Thea Bailey, especially for cancer patients. The main concentration is on relaxation and easing of tension, so that the self-healing powers can be brought to the fore.

It is not a specific anti-cancer treatment, but can aid the road back to good health. Shiatsu is becoming ever more widely available, and it is extremely popular with cancer patients. Of course your practitioner should be somebody who is used to dealing with cancer patients, so that tumours or operation or radiation scars are taken into account.

Circle dancing

Most of the people who come to Bristol for residents' weeks feel decidedly ambivalent about circle dancing when they receive their brochures. For many, it has a distinctly "New Age" feel about it. Also, painful memories of being made to do folk dances at school are still acute in people's minds – at least, those currently over forty.

Another aspect is that very few people have done any kind of dancing at all since they left school. They may wonder what on earth it has to do with coping with cancer anyway. For while it can be easily appreciated that counselling, group discussions and spiritual healing may help patients come to terms with the emotional aspects of cancer, it can be hard to see the connection between cancer care and circle dancing.

Not all residents know what is meant by circle dancing anyway. Is it the same as dancing round a totem pole, or a maypole? Is there some arcane ritualistic significance about it? For all these reasons, very often residents decide in advance that circle dancing is not for them, and make a mental note that they will sit this one out. However, the great majority of residents do end up by joining in, and thoroughly enjoying themselves. Most cancer patients find that they can join in to an extent, however ill they may be, however unfit and whatever stage of recovery they may have reached.

Circle dancing is very different from ballroom dancing in that nobody leads or follows, and you do not have to wear special clothes in order to perform the dances. You do not have to have a marked sense of rhythm, or have learned to dance. The steps are simple, and the idea of doing these movements while together in a circle is that people are enabled to connect with each other in a completely equal way. Circle dancing is not elitist, it does not require a knowledge of complicated steps, and it is a way of establishing unity within the group.

At Bristol, circle dancing comes near the end of the week, when residents have already got to know each other. Mostly, they are surprised at the impact it makes, and how very much they enjoy this part of the programme.

Jane Metcalfe writes about her experiences of circle dancing:

I had never done circle dancing before going to Bristol although of course I had done folk and country dances at school. To me, doing circle dancing was a physical way of expressing the unity we had already come to feel in the group.

The good thing about circle dancing is that you don't have to be good at dancing, or even good at movement. When you do circle dancing, there is almost a feeling of meditation as you move round the circle connecting in turn with each member of the group. It's a way of celebrating life.

On my Bristol week, I found that, in the end, everybody joined in the circle dancing. There were two men there, both rather macho types, a cancer patient and a supporter, who both maintained that there was no way anybody would get them to join in this nonsense. They were both completely set against it.

Yet by the time the evening came round, they were both there, and they appeared in the circle. Both said afterwards that they wouldn't have missed it for anything. Circle dancing to me gives a potent feeling of peace and release. It does us good to move around physically in this manner, and it's a pity that so many of us are put off dance and movement at school.

At its heart, circle dancing is very much about finding your roots, about activating and bringing to the surface your racial memory. In the past, everybody automatically danced – on special occasions, holidays, round the maypole, whenever there was something to celebrate. In Elizabethan and Jacobean times everybody danced, but then dancing became part of the formal court ritual, and passed into an activity which had to be specially learned and was expensive and elitist.

The best thing about circle dancing is that you don't have to be good at it to form a group, or to join a group. Our teachers at Bristol are not professional circle dancing teachers, although these do exist. I would say that the circle dancing evenings are the most enjoyable and convivial aspect of the residents' week, and that people are surprised to get so much out of them. The dances come from all over the world, and everybody can do the steps.

Circle dancing is a way of letting yourself go and of expressing yourself physically. People find they are more graceful, more competent than they expect to be, and of course this gives them confidence.

You may imagine that circle dancing is a highly minority activity only available at places like Bristol, and special centres. In fact, it is increasingly being used for therapeutic and healing purposes, and can have a dramatic impact on feelings and attitudes.

As with other aspects of holistic healing, circle dancing can bring profound emotions to the surface, and allow them to be harmlessly dispelled. The sense of oneness with the group, of not being competitive, of not showing off how good you are at the steps, can impart a sensation of being in harmony both with yourself and with the group. This kind of non-competitive dancing is important in all traditional cultures, and the holistic approach to health care is enabling it to return once more. Circle dancing sessions are now available in several parts of the country, as more people are holding classes, and their deep therapeutic value is being understood.

You can't help but smile when you circle dance, and the activity enables sadness to be danced away.

10
Music and Art Therapy

These two therapies are coming increasingly to the fore as they allow people to express their feelings in a way not normally available, and without the use of words.

Although it is very useful to be able to put what we feel into words, it is also the case that not every profound experience *can* be put into words. If this were the case, there would be no need for visual or musical expressions of deep feeling.

Music therapy

It has always been known that music has the power to evoke strong emotions, and that a particular tune or piece of music can in itself make us feel sad or happy. Certain types of music can also alter emotions and, some people believe, even alter moral sense.

Some types of music can make us feel hyped up, whereas other sounds are relaxing and soothing. It's not for nothing that military music exists, that sonorous organs exist in great cathedrals, or that musicals are the most popular form of live entertainment.

No culture or society has ever been able to do without sounds, and musical instruments have existed since the beginning of civilisation. In the old days, everybody would make their own music naturally, by beating on drums or banging pieces of metal together. Sometimes the sound was harmonious, sometimes jangling and discordant. Nowadays, sound is all around us, but for most of us it is a passive kind of entertainment. We listen to tape and CDs, we go to concerts or to the opera, we perhaps go to church – and all the time we are listening to other people making music.

Music therapy gives you a chance to make your own music. Again, as with circle dancing, you can forget all the painful processes of playing scales, getting pieces exactly right, being singled out for playing out of tune or hitting the wrong notes. With music therapy, there are no "wrong notes" as you are simply expressing yourself through sound.

At Bristol, residents are often initially fearful of the music therapy sessions, because they remember being "bad" at music at school – and may never have touched an instrument since struggling through Grade Three on the piano twenty or thirty years previously.

Of course, some of the Bristol residents are extremely musical, or they may be professional musicians – but these are in the tiny minority. Nervousness around creating sounds is far more common than confidence. As with circle dancing, music therapy sessions give patients an opportunity to express how they are feeling through making sounds. They have instruments which can't fail to make some kind of sound, and everyone can make a joyful noise, even if the result may not be very harmonious in the strict sense of the word.

The harmony from music therapy comes from joining in, from again feeling that you are part of the group, that nobody is judging you, nobody is singling you out. Each one of us is equally proficient when it comes to the therapeutic aspects and any competition is completely ruled out.

Anybody who is interested in this form of therapy can find classes and sessions in their area. The reason that music therapy is offered at Bristol is that it's always good to express exactly how you are feeling and often people cannot unblock their feelings by using words.

You can't block feelings so easily with sound. Music therapy can actually reach the parts where people are holding their deepest feelings, and it is now being used for psychiatric patients, for the seriously mentally ill, and for people who have suffered severe emotional upset. Playing instruments, making noises, gives a potent sense of release and makes it possible to access part of oneself which cannot be expressed in any other way. They now know also that sound waves in themselves can be extremely healing. To an outsider, it may just look as though we're banging drums and making the loudest, most discordant sounds that we can. But actually, everybody feels different, as if a load were off their minds, after music therapy sessions.

Sounds of various kinds are increasingly being used in holistic treatments to enable heightening and alteration of consciousness, and to increase self-awareness. Singing workshops have become enormously popular over the past few years, and their message is similar to that of music workshops: everybody can sing, everybody can make a sound, and everybody can feel better because of it.

As with circle dancing, the sounds that are encouraged in voice and music therapy workshops are the traditional ones, rather than trying to emulate Bach or Beethoven or the voice of Pavarotti. Sound workshops do not exist to enable people to play an instrument or to sing professionally, but to allow people holding pent-up feelings to lose their inhibitions and fearfulness and bring all their being into greater harmony.

Most of us, at least these days, go through life expressing very little of ourselves. It is noticeable that at occasions where there is an opportunity to join in communal singing, such as at church, or Christmas, a majority of people simply stand or sit there and listen, not making a sound. They are afraid that others may consider their voices unattractive. There is enormous self-consciousness surrounding our ability to make sounds, or use our voices in ways other than speaking, and it is part of healing to be able to lose this inhibition.

One of us, Jane Metcalfe, is a professional opera singer and, as such, used to making and being surrounded by sounds which people will actually pay large sums to hear. But, she says, the fact that not all of us have this ability does not mean we should be silent. In fact, she believes that we all can learn to use our voice to the best of its ability and, in this way, express ourselves more freely.

Liz Hodgkinson is one of those people who was always being told to shut up at school, and "pretend" to sing so that the harmony of the other singers, such as it was, would not be disturbed. She was also profoundly inept at playing any musical instrument in a way to please the teachers. Consequently, her music and singing lessons at school held fear and terror. She writes about her Bristol experience of music therapy:

When I saw the array of instruments which we were expected to play, I did not feel very happy about it. For one thing, it all seemed rather childish, and for another, I was not very confident of my ability to make harmonious sounds. I wasn't even sure I could bang a drum or hit cymbals together without deep self-consciousness, so strong was my memory of being shut up for making these noises when a child.

I nervously picked up the instrument which I felt could make least noise and quietly tapped it. I noticed that most of the others did the same, the only one with any confidence being Lily, the professional music teacher, who instantly played a piece of Mozart on her triangle – or whatever she had.

At infant school, even, I had always hated those music lessons where teachers got out the triangles, tambourines and maracas, for the class to try and make a decent sound. But here, of course, everything was different – we were here for therapy, not to be judged on our performing ability.

As the group relaxed, the sounds became louder and more confident. I also was able to relax and enjoy making the sounds. Barbara, our therapist, moved us on and facilitated the session, so that we all got a chance on different instruments, so that we played to each other, played solos, and ensembles.

The session, which lasted about an hour, loosened us up considerably, and taught each of us something more about ourselves and our ability to let ourselves go enough to express what we felt through sound.

Our music therapy session was in the morning, and in the evening, we had a sing-song round the mini-piano. Everybody enjoyed this – it only happens on weeks when somebody is present who actually can play the piano – and even those who professed they couldn't sing, joined in. One of the residents told me what a nice voice I had. As I had always been unceremoniously told to shut up when at school, or whenever I ventured to sing in front of other people, this was a compliment indeed – even if it didn't seem to be true.

One problem with words is that those of us who consider ourselves articulate and verbal will often skate round what we are feeling, and never face the issues squarely. Music and voice therapy enable this block to be bypassed.

Art therapy

Art therapy is now available in some instances on the NHS in Britain, and is coming to be recognised as a valuable way of accessing thoughts and feelings which could not easily come out any other way.

Art therapy has been available at Bristol for many years, and there is a comprehensive selection of paints, pastels and material for making models. At first, as with the music therapy, most people are nervous, but it soon becomes apparent that it is highly enjoyable as well as instructive.

For cancer patients, art therapy provides a means of seeing symbolically where the cancer cells are and what they are doing to the body, mind and spirit. Drawing, painting or making models also enables us to look at our journey, to see where we are going, and where we want to be.

Although art as therapy can be done alone in the home, it is best when a skilled therapist can guide the session, and also help with interpretation. Through this kind of therapy many deep fears can be brought to the surface in a way that might be difficult using language.

It becomes possible to express one's fear of death, one's attitude to relationships, and to oneself.

For Jane Metcalfe, art therapy provided valuable insights. She writes:

When I was a patient at Bristol I drew a picture of my father, which was actually of a great mountain with a stream running down it. The interpretation of this soon became obvious to me: I had always found him unobtainable. This insight was very valuable to my own understanding of how I had related to men in relationships.

One woman with a brain tumour in our group did a clay model of her head and cut the top off so that she could take out the tumour. In fact, a lot of people drew their tumours – this always happens on residents' weeks, and it enables patients to see how they view their tumours, as life-threatening, or something which will gradually disappear and no longer disturb.

Through art therapy, it has become possible to see how the journey has shifted me, and how my self-awareness has grown since cancer was diagnosed.

As with music therapy, you don't have to be artistically gifted to benefit. We can all produce symbols which in their way are as accurate a guide to how we see ourselves as dreams are. Art therapy, of course, can be kept – and it provides a reminder of how we are progressing on our journey.

At residents' weeks, patients are asked to draw or paint themselves as they see themselves – and then, later, as they are when healed. It's always amazing how very different these two pieces of art are. Yet if you asked somebody how they would see themselves when "healed" they would hesitate to describe such a situation to you in words. But mostly, residents find it quite easy to represent this pictorially.

Once you have a concrete image of how it looks to be healed and whole, you can keep this ever by you as something to aim at.

Julie went to Bristol with cervical cancer and, like many others, dreaded the art therapy as she had been told at school that she was not artistic. She says:

> Arriving at Bristol I felt completely comfortable with most of the therapies on offer, but I was dreading the art therapy, as I was certain that everybody would be an artist except me and that I would be in for profound humiliation.
>
> I went with the others up to the art room and found all sorts of materials laid out: papers, paints, string, beads, clay and so on. We were encouraged to use any kind of material we wished. I chose to work outside, and gathered leaves and bits and pieces of twigs and garden stuff. We all showed our creations to each other, and shared feelings about them.
>
> Nobody laughed at what any of the others had done and, as we talked, the meanings behind each piece of art work became clear. I felt that my own painting/collage only showed one facet of myself: the happy, coping, smiling front. Yet I knew there was much more to come – it just hadn't manifested itself yet.
>
> So one evening I took myself off to the art room with another woman who was a professional artist.
>
> I knew that something was bubbling away inside me, and I wanted to try and get it out. Armed with my personal stereo and some favourite tapes, I was soon exploring a theme which had come out in my first painting, when a black line appeared on my current one, as if by accident, and ruined everything. The black just crept across the page. I was really upset and cried and cried. In order to stop the black taking over I started pouring more and more paint over it, using my hands to try and blot out the black.
>
> Eventually, after many more tears and Bob Marley's "Everything's gonna be all right" I cleared the black and had a beautiful pink and white painting. It was my first beautiful painting which I felt confident enough to show people, even a professional artist. It seemed as if a powerful piece of healing had happened – I think the symbolism of the black and my attempts to obliterate it must be obvious – and it had taken me completely by surprise. I am still no artist, but I enjoy drawing now and often use this medium to observe what I'm feeling.

Keeping a diary

This is not strictly speaking an art or music therapy, but it has something in common with each. It is not formally used at Bristol but is certainly recommended, and many people who have never kept a diary before feel the need when a serious crisis such as cancer overtakes them.

True, it's using words, but words which nobody but you will see, so it remains private. It's a very good idea for all cancer patients to keep a diary as soon after diagnosis as possible, to record feelings, emotions, treatments, attitudes.

Again, don't worry that you may not be "literary" or that you may not be able to spell very accurately. Also, don't worry if you have never been very good at expressing yourself in words. The reason for keeping a diary is to have a record of your cancer journey, and to see for yourself how you may be moving on.

When we are depressed, frightened or under great stress, it's easy to imagine that this state is permanent and never changes. In fact, we all have ups and downs, good days and bad days and if you keep a diary over a number of months, you will be able to see how your emotions and attitudes are changing. If, at the same time as starting a diary, you are setting out on a healing journey, you will be amazed at how you change, and how awareness increases.

You will also be impressed by how your assertiveness grows, and how, even in the midst of terrible sorrow and danger the really bad, black moods never last for all that long. We learn, through keeping a diary, that everything passes, and that nothing ever stays totally black for very long.

When keeping a diary, don't worry if your thoughts don't seem to be flowing. Even if you just write down what you did that day, you will still find an accurate indication of how you were feeling when you read it again later.

You don't have to write every day – just when you feel that something is happening, something is changing. And don't only reserve your writing for when you feel depressed. Otherwise, when you read it again, it will seem as though you are always depressed – and that will certainly not be the case.

All these therapies are profoundly healing, all are easy to do, and all provide insights which may be difficult to obtain through other means. Music and art therapy access the right, intuitive side of the brain and let us know what we are really feeling, where we are really at.

The value of keeping a diary is that we have a permanent record of our own progress on our cancer journey. All these therapies allow what is in the deep unconscious to be brought to conscious awareness, and when this happens, true healing can begin.

People often also start to write poetry when they have cancer, even if they have never done this before. Jane Metcalfe writes about her experience of writing poetry as a therapy.

I used to love writing poetry as a child but, after some of my poems were rejected by my English teacher, I stopped doing this, feeling my poems weren't good enough. During the first few months of my recovery from cancer, however, I started to try to express myself through poetry again and was able to release my fears and many of the confused feelings which came up in me. Lots of cancer patients begin to write poetry and, in a way, this can be seen as a validation of themselves, a celebration of still being alive. Whenever I feel sad, stuck or elated, I find a poem just pops out! I hardly ever show these to anybody, but that's not the point. It is my secret way of communicating to myself how I feel.

11

The Talking Cures

Group work and counselling

Group work is very important indeed for cancer patients, as a diagnosis of cancer can be extremely isolating. Suddenly, you feel as if you are completely separated from your friends and family, because this disease sets you apart so much from everybody else you know.

Although the statistics say that one in three people will get cancer, most new patients discover on diagnosis that they don't actually know anybody else who has cancer. Where are all these one in three?

The situation was far worse in the old days, of course, because nobody ever talked about cancer and you might not know that your mother, father, sister or brother, even had it. Maybe they didn't know themselves. Even in the last twenty years or so, when cancer began to be talked about more freely, patients were kept isolated from each other and not encouraged to pool information or feelings. It was as if cancer itself marooned you on an island of isolation, where you were not allowed to talk, not allowed to share – and had to keep all your misery to yourself in case anybody else was affected by it. Now, that has all changed – or at least, it is changing fast. A very reliable American study completed in 1989 showed that joining a group seemed not only to enhance quality of life but also to prolong survival. When comparing like with like, and taking all other variables into consideration such as age, social class and educational levels, breast cancer patients who had been able to join groups lived on average seventeen months longer than others.

It now seems as though the most simple kind of group work is immensely beneficial to cancer patients, and even if it cannot be guaranteed to prolong survival rates, it certainly helps patients to avoid their stress and worry turning into actual mental illness – a common related problem with cancer.

The first recognised self-help groups were those started by Alcoholics Anonymous in America in the thirties, where people who shared a serious problem could come together and, in the safety of the group, try to find ways of recovering and becoming sober. Now, the idea that people can help themselves recover from actual illnesses is growing fast.

Michael Stuart, information officer for CancerLink, a nationwide network of cancer support and self-help groups, says:

Since about 1982, people affected by cancer have created a movement of cancer self-help groups and support groups. There are now over 500 such groups in the UK, with seventy new ones forming each year. These groups vary widely, just as the impact of cancer varies from person to person. The most common aims are: to provide emotional support, practical information and to enable people to live positively with the best possible quality of life.

Whether partners, family and friends are supportive or not, they each have a different perspective from the person with cancer, and there may be issues affecting each relationship which cannot easily be discussed. Cancer support groups, by contrast, offer the opportunity to be with people who are experiencing or who have been through a similar situation and issues. Support is usually offered in a non-directive way. People are allowed to express and explore their feelings in a safe way, without the listener imposing his or her own experience or advice. For some people, just seeing others with "their" cancer who are alive and well offers hope from which to take heart. Almost all groups also offer support to family and friends of people with cancer, and those who have become bereaved.

Jane Metcalfe writes:

Cancer self-help groups can be of immense value to cancer patients starting out on their search for the right therapies. Often groups have more healing potential than almost any other kind of therapy: they are enormously empowering, and they are the greatest success story to come out of the self-help cancer care movement of the past decade. I am so enthusiastic about the value of patient groups that I can't stress enough how powerfully they work.

Groups work on the principle that a problem shared is a problem halved. They can replace, to some extent, the community spirit or close family ties, which used to exist in our society; we hardly know our neighbours and we can go down the street for weeks without anybody speaking to us. When we get cancer, we feel even more isolated and alone, and also frequently we feel that we are suffering from profound ignorance.

We tend to think we know something about cancer, until it strikes, and then we feel helpless. We don't know a thing! We have no idea what sort of tumour we've got, whether we have any chance of recovery, or what sort of treatment might be best. Suddenly, all of our knowledge, if we had any in the first place, seems to leave us.

This is where groups are most helpful. You can ask any cancer question you like, however trivial it may seem, things you would probably hesitate to ask even your oncologist, and somebody in the group may be able to offer enlightenment. At the very least, even if nobody knows the answer, your question will spark off a discussion. Groups are mostly patient-led, but there is a growing band of health professionals interested in complementary approaches who often attend groups, and speakers may be invited to talk on a variety of subjects. This can be helpful when a medical question arises.

Knowledge casts out fear and, within the group, we all become far more knowledgeable than we were before. The success of the group movement for cancer patients can be judged by the fact that in 1979 there were just four or five support groups in existence in the UK for cancer patients, whereas now there are around 500 – and the numbers are growing all the time.

For some people, the idea of joining a group of strangers just does not appeal. Following the shock of a cancer diagnosis, you may need time to decide whether the group experience is for you or not.

In contrast to many people's assumption that a group of people with cancer must be gloomy and depressing, they are very often the opposite: they are frequently social occasions full of activity, laughter and people enjoying each other's company. It is, after all, unusual to meet a group of people who believe in living life to the full, and making the most of every day. It is not uncommon to hear members say that cancer was the best thing that happened to them, as it provided the impetus to re-evaluate what was important to them, and live life accordingly from then on.

As we have tried to stress throughout this book, cancer affects not just the patient but those around them as well. Joining a group can be as valuable for the supporter or partner as for the actual patient, to aid understanding and appreciation of the crisis that has occurred. At Bristol, as much care is taken of the supporters as of the patients. Supporters' needs are often neglected, and they also need the chance to voice their feelings and recognise that even though they are not the ones who are ill, they deserve support as well.

When you feel ready, take your partner or a supportive friend along with you, and give a group a go. You may feel unable to share your experience initially, but hearing others tell their story can encourage you to open up.

Here is a vivid example of how cancer can be a transformational experience not just for the patient, but for the partner as well:

Tony went with his wife to Bristol during the final stages of her illness in 1993. Even though his wife died shortly afterwards, he has found lasting inspiration from his time at the Centre. He says:

To put things into perspective, we had enjoyed forty-three years of happiness together, and we had always felt we were strong enough as a partnership to cope with any eventuality. Fortunately, when we went to Bristol we did not realise that Joan was quite so close to death: in fact, it seemed that several of the other participants that week were closer than she. The Bristol experience was a time of transformation for both of us, but particularly for me. We both came away feeling greatly uplifted and, if possible, closer than we had been before.

I nursed Joan at home during those last weeks and I can honestly say it was as happy a period as we had ever known together. We had a bundle of laughs, which gave me the inspiration and strength to enjoy those weeks to the full, and to endure the succeeding time to the present day.

As a result of his experience at Bristol, Tony has now become a staunch member of Bristol's Patients and Supporters' Panel, formed in 1993 to help with the Centre's work.

Some groups are based in hospitals; a few hold their meetings in members' houses. Most, though, are based on neutral ground. It is best to look for the groups in your area through CancerLink's excellent self-help support group directory which is updated every year. (See Useful Addresses.)

Many groups actually offer complementary therapies such as massage, healing and reflexology free of charge. Others also include social occasions and outings, hold functions, parties and other events. If there is no group in your area, you may consider starting one. There will be plenty of takers, as in some areas of the country, there are still not enough groups in existence.

Lorna is one of the founder members of the Solihull Cancer Support Group. She went to Bristol in 1982, in the original Downfield Road days, having been given a poor medical prognosis for breast cancer. At that time, there was no support available at all, and she felt very isolated. She says:

My "Bristol experience" gave me love, hope and the will to live. Sharing with others was so important. I had the idea to start a local support group, but didn't know how to go about it. Then, as these things happen, I was going on holiday to Spain, and got chatting at the airport to a woman who, by a strange coincidence, had had a lumpectomy and was going down to Bristol! Ruby and I became firm friends and we visited a group at Leamington Spa that was already running. Eventually we were joined by three others, and together we started our group in Solihull.

We believe that hugs and love are the most valuable things we offer. People are always apprehensive when they first walk through the door, but we make sure they don't go away feeling lost and alone. We just love them for being human beings. However, we can't be all things to all people, so we laugh a lot and try not to dwell on the negative.

Lorna's group meets fortnightly and there is always spiritual healing available. There is also foot massage and three trained counsellors can be consulted if necessary. All these services are free to group members. Individual support is offered in between times: "When people are diagnosed, they don't go home and die tomorrow," Lorna says. "They have to live with their cancer. We believe in our group that caring, sharing and giving love are the greatest healers of all."

All groups have their own particular dynamic, depending on the personality of those running the group, and the members at any one time.

CancerLink offers extensive help for anybody interested in starting a group, free of charge. You can contact CancerLink at the address on page 136.

Liz Hodgkinson adds:

I could never have appreciated the impact of group work for cancer patients until I joined one myself, at Bristol. Although at first everybody was nervous and rather suspicious and on guard, this broke down almost instantly, and we all became like old friends within a matter of hours.

Initially, everybody tried to put on a brave face. All of the patients looked perfectly normal, and not at all ill. It was impossible to tell at a glance which were the cancer patients and which were the helpers, therapists or supporters.

But as façades crumbled and people could be themselves, emotions, fears, hopes and actual information were shared in a way that would be difficult even with partners and intimate friends. By the end of the week, an enormous amount had been shared, and the group members felt they knew everybody's cancer history closely.

At times, it seemed as though the discussions would never stop. And the group didn't discuss only cancer, by any means. Although formal group discussions took place every day, people also managed in the meantime to talk about politics, sex, children, jobs, attitudes towards music, literature, food, entertaining, feminism – in fact, just about every subject that could be discussed.

But because everybody was there for a reason, the discussions never descended into small talk – the occasion was far too important for that. It was the isolation of being a cancer patient which came out most strongly from every person there. The experience of being in a group was unanimously felt to be by far the most important aspect of the week in residence.

If you feel that sitting around talking about cancer with other patients is not for you, don't feel bad about it. No holistic therapy can be right for everybody, but even if you don't want to talk about your cancer, it can be a good idea to join a group of some kind. This could be a bridge group, flower arranging, or anything where you share a mutual interest with others, and where you may tap into hidden areas of creativity within yourself. Sharing interests, hobbies and ideas gives a sense of community, of belonging, and whatever you can do to increase this and reduce the feeling of isolation and being alone with your stress and fear, will help the healing process.

Counselling

Cancer counselling is also increasingly being recognised as important, possibly essential. Counselling is different from group work in that you are one-to-one with a skilled therapist.

Many people mistakenly imagine that if you go "into therapy" this must mean there is something wrong with you, that you have a deep-seated "problem" which will be difficult to sort out. There is still a lingering feeling that therapy is only for "nutters".

When we are faced with a life-threatening illness that we can't easily share with our nearest and dearest, it can help immeasurably to be able to talk through our feelings and emotions with somebody who has empathy but who is detached and who will not make any judgments, or react personally to what we have said.

Some people maintain that counsellors are all a waste of time, and that we'd be better off talking to our families, partners and friends. Well, we can do this as well of course – nobody is suggesting that counselling replaces intimate or supportive talk with those who are near to us and know us best.

Counselling comes in addition to this and gives an opportunity to talk about things that we might hesitate to mention to those near to us, for fear of hurting them, or for fear of their reaction. We may also feel that those around us are actually causing our problems, or at least contributing to them.

Those who are emotionally attached to us often react very strongly to certain bits of information. They may not listen with that "unconditional positive regard" which is the stated aim of all genuine counsellors. Also, even if they are able to give this regard, they may not be very good at listening which is, above all, what a counsellor is trained to do.

Families and friends often start talking about themselves instead of listening to you. Also, they may become impatient, remember past misdeeds and in many ways make you feel even worse than you did before.

If your family and friends are supportive of your cancer, then you can of course talk to them as well. But one thing that emerges overwhelmingly from residents' weeks at Bristol is that partners, children, parents are by no means always supportive – and they may even be the very last people with whom you can explore your deepest fears and worries concerning your cancer.

Talking to a trained counsellor, by contrast, gives you the opportunity to explore every emotion which might come up, get it out into the open and examine it. Their job is not to "cure" us of our neuroses, or to tell us what to think or what might have gone wrong in our past.

In counselling, the client does all the talking, and the job of the counsellor is to reflect back what has been said, for clarification. It all proceeds from the client, and the job of the counsellor is to aid access to deep and often hidden fears and emotions.

The point is that when faced with a cancer diagnosis, all kinds of issues which were once buried may burst through to the surface, unannounced and without giving us any strategies for dealing with them. This is because, for most people, cancer is the most severe crisis that can happen, and as such it throws everything else in our life into a sharp relief. Cancer itself can increase awareness – and also bring to the surface long-suppressed emotional pain and trauma which in itself may seem to have nothing to do with the illness.

We may find we are holding long-term resentments and hostilities against those who no longer have the power to hurt us. The resentment won't be bothering them, but it will continue to affect us adversely. There is some evidence to suggest that at least one cause of cancer is long-held resentment, which eventually may affect our physical system. All emotional burdens eventually have a physical outcome, which is why it makes sense to try to free ourselves from them.

Elizabeth had already begun a self-help programme after a diagnosis of breast cancer before she attended Bristol for an introductory day in 1986. She had not originally included counselling in her programme, feeling that as she had not had any dramatic or obvious problems, she wasn't a candidate for it. She says:

> I didn't have a bad home, and all the clichés about needing help if you had a difficult upbringing made me feel I didn't have the right to have help of this kind. But going to the Centre for the first time, I had a session with a counsellor who made me feel I was valuable enough to deserve help. We discovered together that my early home life had not been as idyllic as I liked to imagine, and that there was actually an oppressive atmosphere in my home background.
>
> It seemed that I had never had a proper chance to grow up and I realised that, later on, I was afraid to jeopardise relationships by growing up or changing. I saw that I had quite a lot to work on and, after coming home from the Centre, I went to the Chelsea Pastoral Foundation, where I found a counsellor I could work with regularly. The Bristol counsellor had given me the confidence to realise that I was actually worth having help, and I came to discover that having cancer seemed minor compared to the emotional difficulties of getting on with everyday life.

Whenever we ask: why me? on learning that we have cancer, this can set in motion a train of thought which reminds us of hurts and slights we may be harbouring that go back years. One patient on a residents' week remembered that, as a small child, she had wanted to be an actress, and had received nothing but hoots of derision from her family when she shyly announced it.

She had not thought about this for years, but was now certain that the derision of her family had meant that she never did what she really wanted to, and never had enough self-confidence to lead the life of her choice. Her cancer gave her the chance to examine and work through this memory.

The stress of cancer can force us to take a possibly initially painful look at all the things which may not be right in our lives and ask ourselves what we can do about them. American psychologist Lawrence Le Shan sees cancer as a turning point, but sometimes we may need help to make that turning, or to see exactly where to make the turn.

There is some evidence to suggest that cancer patients who have had counselling do better than those who try to manage without. Talking in a safe setting, whether in a group or with a therapist, enables people to face what they may have suppressed before.

Counselling can help us to cope with the painful feelings which insist on forcing themselves to the surface however much we try to keep them down and under wraps. It can enable us to identify our needs.

Throughout this book we have emphasised the importance of singing your own song. This is all very well, but may be difficult if you don't know how to sing your song, or even what your song is. Finding and singing your own song may be particularly difficult for women who may never even have considered that they had a song to sing, but simply assumed their role in life was to look after others and be there for them.

When cancer strikes, we need somebody to be there for us – but there might not be anybody around to play that role. Expert counselling can help cancer patients to deal with the stress which now accompanies their lives and to find effective ways of managing it. At first, counselling may be disturbing and painful, as sometimes in order to heal, we have to go through the pain and let it float away. It can also help people to face their feelings of helplessness and vulnerability and give a renewed zest for living. Once we have faced our pain, we may be able to start living again freed from its hold.

Counselling can also help to establish goals, to discover what these are and to find effective ways of meeting them. Having goals can help cancer patients to overcome their fears and then shift the emphasis of their lives away from the illness and into more productive and creative areas. It can help through a "stuck" patch and allow us to find new strengths.

Very many cancer patients believe that they have to face all the difficulties and problems by themselves and that to admit they may need help, that they simply can't cope with all the emotions that arise, is a sign of weakness.

But in fact, the ability to ask for help is a sign of strength, an indication of a new assertiveness. The authors of this book have both experienced entirely positive outcomes from expert counselling and one, Jane Metcalfe, decided to train herself as a counsellor after being on the receiving end. In some ways, those who have had to cope with cancer themselves may make better cancer counsellors than others – but this is not essential. However, it is often a personal crisis which gives the motivation to train as a counsellor.

It is not uncommon for cancer patients who have been to Bristol, and benefited from the holistic therapies on offer there, to train themselves as counsellors so that they can help others through this crisis. In this way, cancer patients can provide a kind of chain of help for each other and, if they train as counsellors, this means that the help is put on a professional basis.

We can attest to the dramatic difference that counselling can make. The feeling you are left with after successful counselling is that with every step you take, heavy black overcoats are falling off you and you are becoming freer and lighter.

Cancer patients need to feel as "light" as possible in order to cope with their illness.

12

Meditation

Meditation has always been considered important at Bristol and, although it has things in common with breathing and relaxation, it is subtly different from either. It basically consists of being able to still the mind to stop and focus the noisy traffic of thoughts which bother us during our waking hours, and to provide an oasis of calm during the busiest day.

At residents' weeks at Bristol, there are moments for group meditation throughout the day. At first, many patients – particularly those who have not tried meditating before – find it hard to sit still without apparently doing anything for even five minutes, but towards the end of the week, meditation sessions have usually become popular with everybody.

Meditation sounds easy: all you do is to sit still in a chair, listen to a soothing tape or voice, and empty your mind until you go into a quiet, peaceful realm where you experience lovely colours, sights and sounds.

This is how meditation is described, and certainly some people achieve some kind of blissful or transcendental state during their first experience of meditation. However, these people are the exception.

For most, meditation is quite difficult and may be rather boring. Some people find it actually disconcerting, as all kinds of unwelcome thoughts can rise up unbidden to the surface. Five minutes can seem an awfully long time when you are just sitting still, and trying hard to concentrate on a candle flame, or on a mantra such as 'Om'.

During meditation sessions, people often find they think of anything but the peaceful realm of stillness and calm they are supposed to be entering. Instead, they compile shopping lists, wonder whether they've turned the gas off, start to worry about whether they've paid a particular bill or will have enough money to last them the month, or whether they've said anything to offend their nearest and dearest. And, try as they might, they cannot seem to stop these thoughts from coming. For such people, meditation seems to be a waste of time.

And yet, all spiritual paths, all religions, have a central place for meditation or prayer in their observances. In ancient yogic traditions, adherents are supposed to get up at around 4 am, the so-called "hour of nectar" when the world is still and hustle and bustle has not yet begun, and concentrate their thoughts on the pure and peaceful aspects of themselves.

The idea is that gradually, through meditation, waste or unwelcome thoughts will vanish and in their place will come positivity and healing.

Most of the patients who come to Bristol have not experienced formal meditation, even though it has been in Western culture since the dawn of Christianity, in modern times thousands of people have gained from it. In order to gain the maximum from your meditation sessions, we are told, you need to practise it at least twice a day, for twenty minutes.

What an ordeal! When patients come to Bristol, they are often nervous and suspicious of meditation. At first, the majority does not look forward to the meditation sessions that are held every day. This is noticed time and again on residents' weeks and points to an important truth: meditation, like any other thing in life worth doing, has to be learned, and it takes time to establish the habit.

We are not saying that meditation is for everybody – but all residents at Bristol are urged at least to give it a try, because regular meditation alters consciousness.

Jane Metcalfe's experiences of meditation:

I had never done any meditation before going to Bristol, and I must say I found it extremely difficult. At first, I don't think I understood what it meant to clear the thoughts. The paradox is that whenever you try to clear your thoughts, you find you can't.

My experience was that meditation takes a lot of practice and, initially, it can seem counter-productive, as all the thoughts you don't want to rise to the surface insist on coming there. Then you have to deal with them. My own recommendation is that people who find meditation difficult should find some suitable classes they can go to, as meditation is always far easier and more powerful in a group.

At the Centre, there is a choice of different types of meditation. There is meditation on a candle flame, which is probably the most popular type; the sort of meditation where you are slowly counted down; and meditation on a mantra, that is, a special word or phrase used mentally to help you focus.

I think what all cancer patients have to do is to find the system of meditation which suits them, and persevere. I would say you need to give it a good try before you can decide for sure that it's not doing anything for you. I now find I can meditate best on a text or phrase which means something to me.

All meditation really means is a kind of silent prayer, and if you're a Christian, you can always go into a church, find a quiet corner – and spend a few minutes silently collecting your thoughts.

Penny Brohn also found meditation difficult initially. In her book on the Bristol Programme, she writes that she didn't manage to achieve much of the inner tranquillity held up as the goal of meditation, and she felt unsure of herself and also rather embarrassed. She confesses that when she first tried meditation by herself, she did it lying on the floor with her foot against the door in case anybody came in and found out what she was doing.

It is sad that to be caught at meditation may seem more embarrassing than to be caught masturbating.

The whole point of meditation is to become the detached observer, to be able to see yourself as an actor on a stage, playing your part, but in a sense, at one remove. Once we are able to detach ourselves from our thoughts, we then become able to detach equally from our worries, fears, anxieties and tensions. They can flood out of the system as a core of peace comes in.

Meditation has the physical effect of lowering adrenaline levels in the system and slowing down brainwaves, thus enabling the creative, healing mode to take over. Meditation can also help to bring the two halves of the brain, the left, or logical, rational side and the right, the intuitive, feeling side, together so that they can work in harmony.

Mind machines have established that whenever there is harmony in human life, there is a strong connection between these two halves of the brain. We need both – and we need to utilise both in our healing of ourselves. Meditation is a way of bringing both the conscious and the unconscious aspects of ourselves into harmony.

You may be convinced that meditation is a good idea, but how do you get started, and how do you continue? The first thing to understand about meditation is that it needs regular discipline. Residents who come to Bristol are made very aware of this, that it's essential to set aside certain times for meditation, and that, ideally, these should be the same times each day, so that daily or regular meditation is built into your everyday life.

The second important aspect is that you have to find a form of meditation which suits you. Specific kinds have been developed at Bristol, but these are the ones the therapists themselves practise and have found to work. You may find others. There is silent meditation, meditation with a commentary to help you to focus your thoughts, meditation with incense, meditation with chanting, meditation alone or meditation in a group.

When trying to find a form of meditation which suits you, you have to decide what sort of person you are. If you are a rather exotic, sensual kind of person, you may prefer incense and chanting. Chanting itself can powerfully alter consciousness, although for some people it seems both weird and unnecessary.

The Sivananda Yoga Centre, which has published several books on yoga practice, has a form of meditation which consists of chanting names of ancient gods and goddesses in front of an altar strewn with flowers and images of gods such as Vishnu, Krishna, and Buddha. Tapes are available.

The Brahma Kumaris practise a very different form of meditation which needs no props. Instead, you keep your eyes open and fix your gaze on the person – usually a white-saried woman – who is conducting the meditation. The Brahma Kumaris' form of meditation is silent, although sometimes tapes of music are used to get people into a quiet frame of mind. BKs meditate at four in the morning, and at certain times of the day to practise what they call "traffic control" – a couple of minutes taken out of whatever else you may be doing to still the busy traffic of the mind, and calm you down when you may be under stress. It's valuable "time out" from daily activities, and is particularly beneficial if you are facing a tough challenge, or possible bad news.

Siddha Yoga meditation is very different, consisting of chanting and very long stretches of meditation during which people hyperventilate, cry out and make strange noises. It is not everybody's cup of tea, but may suit those who like a "happening" in their meditation.

Those practising transcendental meditation meditate on a mantra. Everybody is supposed to be given their own special and secret mantra which they repeat over and over again to induce an internal stillness and peace. In fact, most people have the same, or at least, a similar, mantra. TM has to be practised twice a day, morning and evening, for twenty minutes, and, worldwide, it is the most popular form of meditation to come from the East.

The point of meditating on a mantra, or a candle flame, is that it helps us to distance ourselves from our thoughts. Whenever thoughts come in to trouble us, as they will, we can instantly return to the mantra or the object we are meditating on. In his book *Teach Yourself to Meditate*, meditation teacher Eric Harrison reminds us that the mind constantly wants entertainment, and this is why it will try to keep diverting to other, more interesting matters.

Eric Harrison lists the advantages of meditation as being able to sleep well, rise early and be in a good mood all day. He adds that meditation enables us to have more energy, become healthier, to think and work more efficiently, and to enjoy more. It is a state of being both relaxed and aware.

But it does take practice. Cancer patients may have a greater reason to meditate than those who are well, because they have a powerful motivation to heal their illness. Eric Harrison mentions in his book that he is often asked whether meditation can cure cancer. His reply is that meditation *supports* a cure; in other words, it is perfect complementary medicine, as it assists the natural healing process of the body.

It may, adds Harrison, be the crucial factor which helps a person overcome cancer, but it is unlikely to be the sole cause of their becoming tumour-free.

The particular health benefits of meditation – and these have now been well researched – are that meditation relieves muscular tension, works to lower high blood pressure, and stimulates the immune system and the production of white blood cells – vital for overcoming cancer.

Meditation can also increase blood circulation in the digestive tract, skin and brain. It affects hormonal activity to its betterment and, in general, acts as a naturopathic treatment to bring the whole body and mind into harmony.

The more stressed you are, the more adrenaline is likely to be racing round the system, and the more you are in need of meditation. Bristol believes that meditation practice is essential to set the body and mind's own healing powers in motion, and they recognise that this can be hard when everything – mind, body, spirit – is under great stress. And that prevents healing from taking place.

Can deep healing happen through meditation? It is the case that every cancer patient will, sooner or later, come across some "miracle cure", and hear the story of a sufferer who was told there was nothing more that could be done, and so decided to give up all and go into a monastery, or into a retreat to die.

A few years later, however, they are perfectly well and happy. Their tumour has disappeared. But you don't have to go into a monastery to bring about a miracle cure. One cancer patient was told that he had, at most, three months to live, as his tumour had spread and was in any case inoperable. He was in a deep state of shock, but he decided that it was now or never, and that he would do what he had always wanted to do. He was at the time working in a senior position in a bank, and had always been quite successful in his job. However, his private life was not so happy.

As he had such a short time to live, he thought it was time for him to enjoy himself as never before. He divorced his wife, and escaped to Switzerland with his young lover. You can guess the rest of the story. More than ten years later, he is perfectly well and there is no sign of the tumour. He and his lover managed to get jobs in Switzerland, when it became clear he wasn't going to die after all – and they are still there, not rich, but happy because they are together.

Eventually, this man decided to sing his own song – and it worked. His life became a form of meditation, and he managed to get rid of the stress and worry which had at least contributed to his cancer even if it had not directly caused it.

Most of us are under stress, even if we don't realise it, but cancer puts us under even more stress. Eric Harrison points out that the cause of most stress is blocked or frozen emotion which occurs when we live a lie, when we do not sing our own song, for whatever reason.

If the emotions which are blocked and buried can't come out as emotions, they may well come out as illness. The more blocked and buried the emotions are, the more serious the illness is likely to be. And emotions are not just "in the mind". They intimately affect the body, as they cause stress hormones to be released which put the body out of equilibrium. The more powerful the emotions which can't be allowed to rise to the surface, the more serious the illness that results.

When we meditate, we become able to see what thoughts are causing negative emotions, what is blocking us. As we become detached from these thoughts, we can see them for what they are – poisons that are contaminating our minds and bodies. We start to be able to see the difference between healthy and unhealthy thoughts and emotions. And gradually, we become able to weed out those which are not doing us any good.

If we feel angry with somebody, who is this hurting: them or us? Clearly, ourselves. Unless we vent our anger on the person we feel deserves it – and this rarely happens in polite society – we keep our rage to ourselves. We may feel that our blood "boils" when we read of some injustice in the newspaper or see it on television, but what good, really, does that anger do?

It only puts our own blood pressure up – it doesn't improve the situation. Once we start meditating, we gradually become aware of old, unhelpful patterns of thought and reactions. We may discover that as soon as we start to think of a parent, resentment rises up.

As time goes on, though, it becomes possible to forgive those who have hurt us in the past. And that is where the deep healing process starts. With meditation, though, as with changing to a healthier diet, there may be a healing crisis, a time when all thoughts seem more uncomfortable than before. Initially, meditation may be experienced as discomfort, as thoughts and emotions you imagined you had forgotten all about, as old hurts and slights, force themselves to the surface.

But once they come to the surface, they can be allowed to go and you will no longer feel the hurt and the pain. But it won't necessarily all happen at once. In fact, what you may find is getting rid of one painful layer just causes another to come to the surface. Clearing the mind of negativity is rather like taking tissues out of a box: you take out one, and another pops up until the box is empty. Thoughts, like tissues, are interconnected.

You may successfully rid yourself of something which hurt that happened, say, twenty-five years ago that you have never quite been able to forget, and watch it float away, only to find that not long afterwards something even older and more painful forces its way to the forefront of your mind. Don't worry about it – just watch it happening, as if it were a boil which is going to burst and be rendered harmless any minute. As you go on, ever more pains, slights and problems will rise up, be faced, and disappear.

Then real healing happens and you are able to change your consciousness. You become self-aware, in charge, lighter. Eventually, you become able to connect to everything around you, to become part of it and realise that you are not separate from your surroundings, from other people or from what is happening in the universe. You are, rather, part of it, part of the ebb and flow of life.

Holding on to negative emotions has the effect of distancing us from other people, of blocking out love, compassion and tolerance. We have to realise that other people are here to do their own thing, and that we may well be unable to influence their decisions. We certainly cannot undo anything which happened in the past – we can only decide not to be adversely affected by it any more.

Whenever something causes you undue pain, then instead of trying to block it out, go with it and see where the thoughts lead you. Through meditation can come a dramatic degree of self-realisation, of understanding that you can be responsible for your own thoughts, and for freeing yourself from old, unhelpful emotions and reactions.

In order for genuine healing to take place, the mind has to separate itself from all negativity. This is not easy to do, and always elements of negativity will surface. None of us is perfect, but we can all be on a journey towards greater self-awareness. Through meditation, says Eric Harrison in his book, we become able to see what our thoughts are doing for us, whether they are helping us or hindering us. Also, when we become clearer in our minds, we can take a more active part in our own healing programme. We can make decisions which are going to be for our own good, not just accede to whatever other people might want for us.

Very often, to be given a death sentence from the doctor works to enable us to take complete stock of ourselves and our lives. Eric Harrison recommends two to three hours' meditation a day for cancer patients, and says that whereas a little meditation helps a little, a lot of meditation helps a lot. In fact, it is probably only through deep meditation that genuine changes and improvements can be made.

Getting started on your own

It is undoubtedly easier to meditate in a group than on your own, as group dynamics make the experience much more powerful and also enable you to finish the session, in much the same way as exercise classes or anything initially difficult are so much easier when a group is headed by a teacher who keeps you going.

If you can find a meditation class which suits you, then this can form part of your own complementary therapy. But it may not be possible, or you may be too ill at times actually to go to a class. But never imagine that if you can't get to your class, this means you can't meditate. It often helps to find a class at first, so that you can establish the habit before deciding to do it on your own.

Although most yoga groups and religious organisations hold that the best time to meditate is very early in the morning, this may not be practical for cancer patients, or those who have very busy schedules. You also have to determine your own body rhythms and inclinations. If you are a slow starter in the morning, you may find that this is your best time to meditate. But if you spring out of bed fully awake the minute the alarm goes off, or even before, you may find you are in too much of a hurry to spend time meditating in the morning. For you, a quiet time in the evening would be better.

If you are not following a specific spiritual path, it doesn't much matter what time of the day you decide to meditate. The important thing is that you set aside time to do it every day. Even if you don't seem to be able to set aside special meditation sessions, you will still find there are many pockets of time during the day when you've got nothing to do, such as being on a train, stopping at traffic lights, waiting for supper.

The important thing is to make it a habit, so that it is built into daily life as much as cleaning teeth or putting on socks.

Spiritual Healing

Spiritual healing plays a central part in the Bristol programme. All cancer patients who come as residents are invited to have at least one spiritual healing session, which takes place in the chapel.

It will be remembered that the Centre began as a spiritual healing ministry, and grew out of this approach. In a sense, all of Bristol's other therapies are informed by this foundation of spiritual healing.

Pat Pilkington describes how spiritual healing came into her life, and that of her husband, after working in the same diocese in the Church of England as the Rev. Tim Tiley, an unconventional vicar who enabled them to see a new dimension of healing, and was the original inspiration for their own healing ministry, the forerunner of the Cancer Help Centre.

It seemed to us that the Church was full of dispirited clergy, trying to put over a message which was, in many ways, unheeded and out of date. It was like pushing a large boulder uphill. Tim pointed out that the Church's hierarchy had always made it difficult for healers, but that compassion – unconditional, non-judgmental love – was the most important thing any spiritual person could offer.

Initially, as with many of the other therapies on offer, patients may feel somewhat suspicious of spiritual healing, perhaps equating it with faith healing, or with spiritual*ist* healing. But the great majority of patients, if not all, come away with the feeling that this has perhaps been the most valuable session of all, however sceptical or nervous they may have been previously.

In fact, spiritual healing has always played a significant part in complementary approaches to cancer. During the late seventies, Lieutenant-Colonel Marcus Macausland, who founded the charity New Approaches to Cancer, used to hold spiritual healing sessions at his London house. There, spiritual healers would gather, and gently lay hands on the cancer patients present, transferring their energy and sending out positive, loving thoughts. At the time, this approach was considered extremely cranky, and few saw how it could possibly help cancer patients. There was no doubt that they felt better for it, and that in many instances, "something" did happen. Since those days, spiritual healing has become "respectable", and is ever more widely available. Increasing numbers of medical doctors now have spiritual healers in their surgeries, and say that these healers are always extremely popular.

You may wonder what happens during a spiritual healing session, if you have had no experience of this. The answer is, often, very little as such. The spiritual healer may lay hands on you – in the Christian ministry, spiritual healing is known as the "laying on of hands" or may not even touch you. Then you as the patient, may feel a definite physical reaction coming from the healer. Sometimes this is experienced as heat, or warmth, sometimes as vaguer sensations going through the body. Sometimes, you may twitch and shake. But it is never anything of which to be afraid. Spiritual healers are people who understand that, whenever we become seriously ill, there is some deep disharmony within the spirit, or the non-physical aspect of humans. It is this non-physical aspect which is addressed, not by dwelling on it but by seeing the inner perfection that is within us all.

Such healers focus on the spirit, rather than the body. When a healer tunes into a patient, he or she acts as a channel for healing energy. Healers provide a kind of jump-lead which can enable healing to take place, but this healing may happen on a very subtle level.

There is not universal agreement among spiritual healers as to exactly what they are tapping into when there is this potent transfer of energy, but they all agree that the healing power comes through, rather than from them.

Most of the patients who come to Bristol are impressed and also surprised by their spiritual healing sessions. Expecting something weird and strange, they can be reassured to discover how normal it is, and how much like ordinary, everyday people, spiritual healers are. They are not people dressed in weird robes who mutter strange incantations over you, but are simply individuals, men and women, who have discovered a healing power within themselves, and want to pass this on. Canon Christopher Pilkington had been for many years aware of some healing power within himself before he began his healing ministry.

There was no doubt of its popularity when it was established in Bristol and, as it gradually loses its strange image, it is becoming more respectable all the time. At Bristol, great care is taken so that the spiritual healing sessions take place in a setting which is calm and peaceful. This is why the Centre is glad to have a real chapel in the building.

Spiritual healers are adept in the art of visualisation. Instead of seeing a sick and ill person before them, they visualise you being in perfect health. They also themselves go into "healing" mode, which means that their brainwaves slow down and they become completely calm and relaxed themselves.

In fact, unless the spiritual healer is himself or herself calm and peaceful, healing cannot take place. Genuine spiritual healers prepare themselves for sessions by making sure they are not hyped-up, but are able to transfer the peace that they feel to their clients.

Most modern spiritual healers do not see themselves as supplanting the work of orthodox doctors, but complementing it and enabling healing to take place on levels other than the purely physical.

You may wonder whether there is really anything in spiritual healing, or whether the effect is simply placebo, and just makes you feel better without actually doing anything more. In fact, in recent years, a large number of laboratory experiments have taken place using spiritual healers, and it does seem as though the best of them have some special gift which can affect matter.

Experiments in America have shown that spiritual healers have the ability to affect the germination of seeds, in that they can speed it up. There has also been some research into absent healing, where healing thoughts and energy are sent out to those who cannot be physically present – and of the recipient picking up the energy at the same time as it is being sent out.

Very often, it takes a severe crisis such as cancer for people to be able to accept spiritual healing. At such times, people become ready to accept all kinds of help that they may have rejected or scorned when well.

Spiritual healing has been found to be invaluable for cancer patients, and is highly recommended as an aspect of complementary care as soon after diagnosis as possible. You do not have to adhere to any particular belief system to benefit from spiritual healing, but you may perhaps prefer to request a healer from your own faith, if this is important to you.

In a sense, we can all be spiritual healers, in that we can all lay a gentle hand on somebody's shoulder, or give their hand a loving squeeze. In its simplest form, spiritual healing is an extension of a mother kissing a child's wound better. We have all felt the power of this as children, and we can treat ourselves to the grown-up version. Sometimes, spiritual healing can accomplish miracles, but at the very least, it provides a loving touch, somebody concentrating on you and wishing you all the very best, and that can't be bad. Certainly, these days nobody should ever consider spiritual healing peculiar, or take any notice of people – who are usually speaking out of complete ignorance and prejudice – who warn you against this practice, and of charlatans and quacks who promise to cure you.

No spiritual healer should ever hold out a promise of a cure, or that they can shrink tumours. This may happen, but it is more likely that they can help you to feel whole and healed within yourself, so that self-healing on many levels can take place.

After all this, you may wonder what on earth it is going to cost you to get well as a cancer patient. For although orthodox treatments don't, in the UK at least, cost you anything – and in other countries they can be taken care of through medical insurance – complementary treatments usually have to be paid for, and it can all add up inexorably.

Although very few complementary practitioners overcharge, of course, all one-to-one and hands-on treatments can be quite expensive. However, many therapists can negotiate lower fees, so do ask. Joining a self-help cancer group will not cost you anything, and therapists often volunteer their services to help cancer support group members as they know that if you are ill, you are less likely to have money to spare just when you need the therapies most. Cancer patients often are, or at least, become, poor, because they may no longer be able to work to earn money.

We are not suggesting that every cancer patient books up every single one of the holistic therapies which are on offer at Bristol. The whole point about having such a variety of treatments is that patients can sample them and then see what seems to suit them best.

Even if you can afford at least one – you will be taking part in your own healing process, and this can only improve the quality of your life and make you feel in charge. You must also feel that you deserve it and, once you realise this, it's surprising what you can afford. You have to make getting well an absolute priority.

There are "umbrella" organisations who will provide you with details of registered complementary practitioners in your area. (See Useful Addresses.)

Ask at your hospital what kinds of complementary care are available, and whether there is any extra charge. There may not be for cancer counselling, or for spiritual healing. Ever more hospitals are expanding their complementary therapy range, and you may find there is more on offer than you ever expected, and that as a cancer patient you will not have to pay any extra. Find out what is available on the NHS – and you may be surprised that it's more than you imagine. Art therapy, for instance, is now available in some circumstances under the health service.

Some therapists may not make any charge for cancer patients, but make up their income by charging those who are already well. Very many therapists also have a sliding scale of charges, so never imagine that inability to pay means that you can't take advantage of the beneficial therapies outlined in this book. This is where joining a cancer group can be so helpful – you can take advantage of the pooled information and expertise.

If you are nervous about what it is going to cost, remember that you don't have to book up a huge number of sessions in advance. You can just have one – and see what it feels like.

Note

This introduction to the therapies on offer at Bristol is meant to be just that – an introduction. Whole books have been written on all of these complementary therapies, and if you want to delve any deeper into them before deciding whether they might be for you, please refer to the resource list at the back of the book.

It is not possible to offer every single type of therapy at Bristol, but the Centre has put together the package which seems to be the most beneficial. You may find others which suit you.

Again, this is one of the valuable aspects of joining a patient group. Other members will have had experience of complementary therapies, and can pass on their thoughts and experiences. Of course, what suits one person may not appeal to you, but we can't emphasise enough the importance of accessing the feel-good factor.

14

The Way Forward

We believe that it's not an exaggeration to say that Bristol has dramatically influenced cancer treatments, both orthodox and complementary, world-wide. Bristol doctors and therapists have spoken at conferences all over the world, and have taken the Bristol approach to very many corners of the globe.

Before Bristol, there were basically two distinct and quite separate approaches to cancer care, to the disease which has baffled doctors ever since time began and which continues to baffle them: you could either run the full gamut of orthodox treatment, or, if you were very brave and very assertive, you could take yourself to an alternative clinic. But never the twain could meet.

Mostly, the alternative clinics were expensive, difficult to reach and constituted a completely maverick approach to cancer. The therapies on offer there, as Penny Brohn describes in her book *Gentle Giants*, were often as difficult and as stressful as the orthodox care.

At the Gerson clinic, for instance, which is described in Beata Bishop's book *A Time to Heal*, the régime of raw juices, including liver extract, of coffee enemas and a full-time dedication to a difficult and unenjoyable diet, would daunt all but the most well-motivated person. In her book, Beata describes how she survived the régime, and how her malignant melanoma, which had already developed secondaries, healed completely. She is certain that such a total cure would not have been possible through orthodox treatment. She may well be right – but nobody could say that the régime at the alternative clinics was much like spending a month in a five-star hotel.

Before Bristol, you had to choose – and if you chose the alternative places, you would also risk disapproval for taking yourself off to a weird and probably highly expensive clinic where the treatments were widely considered to be unproven and ineffective, and possibly even harmful.

Bristol's great contribution to cancer care, as we see it, was to integrate the orthodox and the alternative treatments so that patients could do both, and would no longer have to make an agonising choice. Penny Brohn describes how her orthodox specialists washed their hands of her in exasperation when she decided she wanted to try and treat herself – they did not support her in her choice.

She was alone and isolated. In those days – only the late seventies, so not very long ago – there were also very few cancer support groups, there was no cancer counselling, and there was no official recognition of the fact that cancer could be a stressful, fearful, anxiety-making condition as well as one which was difficult to treat.

With cancer, both the diagnosis and the treatment are difficult and painful, and there are no easy answers. Bristol came into being to help cancer patients cope with the great fear that surrounds the disease and the immobility that such fear can often bring.

From the first day it opened its doors, the Bristol Centre has recognised the fact that cancer, being arguably the most serious disease of our time, possibly of all time, presented an opportunity for change, for personal growth, for heightened self-awareness. Patients could be empowered and heal themselves mentally, emotionally and spiritually at the same time as doing whatever seemed necessary to heal the physical condition, the presenting tumour.

It is good to see that, after more than a decade of being considered cranky, strange and ridiculously lovey-dovey, the Bristol message is now being accepted by increasing numbers of orthodox doctors. Very few cancer doctors these days are deaf to the idea that cancer presents an emotional challenge as well as a physical one, and that the psychological impact may be at least as great as the actual tumour – perhaps greater, because for many cancers, at least in the early stages, there is no pain and no problem. Patients may feel perfectly well and fit when they are told they have cancerous cells – and may have experienced no symptoms whatever.

But although Bristol has always concentrated on "gentle" treatments which do the body no harm, at no time have Bristol doctors – and remember that there have always been orthodox-trained doctors at Bristol, and always will be – ever suggested that these could provide a cure in themselves. This would have been arrogant indeed.

The main function of the Bristol therapies has always been to help people handle their stress, and also give the opportunity for patients to strengthen their immune systems by all means possible. The idea was to create a healing milieu, which was also one of love, acceptance and nurturing.

When the Centre first started, this approach was completely new, and the message seemed initially startling. At the time, few orthodox cancer specialists were giving any thought to the possibility that the immune system might be compromised by the toxic treatments, and that to take steps to strengthen the body's own self-healing mechanisms might be a good idea.

It seems logical and sensible once you say it – but, as always, when ideas are new, they tend to be summarily rejected. Now these ideas are no longer so new – and the orthodox world is now taking them on board.

Dr Rosy Daniel (formerly Thomson), the Centre's Medical Director, tells why she became interested in the holistic approach.

It was not that complementary medicine was a "second best" for me, or that I hadn't done well as an orthodox doctor when I started out. I had gained a first class BSc, and had done my professional work in medicine, surgery, obstetrics and psychiatry. However, two key elements made me feel that I did not want to spend my career in orthodox medicine: one was the clear connection between mind and body, and the other was a growing awareness of the devastating emotional gulf as people given conventional treatment were abandoned to their fear, grief and confusion.

I feel it is imperative that twentieth-century medicine seeks to understand the root causes of disease, and how to use the mind and spirit in the recovery process. Most of the health professionals who have worked at Bristol throughout the years have all been people who were dissatisfied with orthodox medicine, as this so often takes away the person's individuality in a mass approach.

Because Bristol patients have, on the whole, been so enthusiastic about the therapies, and about the help they have received, they have taken this message of hope out into the world. They have spoken positively about Bristol to their doctors, to their families and friends, they have started support groups, they have battled and campaigned on Bristol's behalf, they have written letters to the newspapers, they have appeared on television.

The net effect of this, notwithstanding the almost fatal blow of the Chilvers report, is that Bristol-type therapies are now available in many large cancer hospitals. As patient demand increases, so will the availability of the therapies. After all, the NHS, like any business that is consumer-led, has to take notice of its clients' needs and wishes.

Conventional cancer specialists, at least the new generation, have become convinced that there is at least a place for complementary therapies, and the idea that support groups can be helpful is gaining fast. Many important cancer hospitals now have patient support groups, where treatments, approaches and information can be shared and discussed.

At last, at last, the terrible sense of isolation which cancer patients feel is being seriously addressed.

At the time of writing, Bristol still stands proud, and is attracting a new generation of therapists, doctors and helpers. But there are still many who have been there since the beginning, and are as enthusiastic as ever.

The residents' weeks have once again become popular, as have the introductory days, since the public censure of the Chilvers report following the campaign of the Bristol Survey Support Group. The courses are once again full, and the growing interest in the Centre's educational courses for health care professionals is also a testament to the way current thinking is going. But even after so many years, Bristol remains one of the few cancer care clinics of its type in the world. By far the great majority of complementary help centres are day centres only, without the residential facilities we have always felt were such an important part of the Bristol approach.

So what is the way forward? Has Bristol had its day now that complementary therapies are at last accepted by orthodox doctors – or will it continue to be as influential in the nineties as it undoubtedly was in the eighties.

It seems to us that there will always be a place for Bristol. For although ever more hospitals and health centres are offering complementary therapies for cancer patients, these are often sporadic, not always available, not always offered with sufficient conviction, and are liable to be taken away at any minute, should funding or doctors change.

Also, most of the hospitals offering holistic approaches are following Bristol's lead: they have seen that certain therapies make a difference, and for that reason have decided to offer them.

So, at one level, Bristol provides a nerve centre, a place which concentrates holistic and complementary care, which tries it out in a dedicated and committed way, and which can continue to be avant-garde, exploring and evaluating all that is new and promising in psychological and spiritual approaches to one of the most serious life crises anybody can face.

The Centre itself is now attracting patients at an earlier stage of their cancer journey – as we like to call it – rather than after they have been through the full gamut of orthodox treatments and the stress and anxiety which comes from living with cancer for several years. At first, people only came to Bristol, on the whole, when they were told that there was nothing more that could be done – and not wanting to die just yet, they were desperate.

Now, though, they are starting to book up residents' days or weeks at an early stage, so that they can incorporate their orthodox and complementary treatments right from the start. We believe that this combination will offer the best package of cancer treatments currently available.

Another important thing that Bristol does is encourage patients to ask questions about their cancer treatment, such as: what is the evidence that this works? Why can't you operate? Where can I get a second opinion? What will happen to me if I refuse all orthodox treatment? What are the chances of successful treatment? What are the known side-effects of this treatment? Is there anything else that can help me? What about support groups? What do you offer in the way of holistic or complementary treatments? What is actually known for certain about this type of cancer?

Through gaining the courage to ask such questions – which cancer patients, on the whole, did not do before Bristol came into being – you can put yourself in charge, rather than passively accepting what you are told. No doctor knows everything, and even the best cancer specialists have to admit there is much that evades them about the disease.

The team at Bristol doesn't know everything either – but are willing to learn. There is no guidance on specific treatments, no differentiation in the approach between different forms of cancer. So far as Bristol is concerned, cancer is cancer, and the emotional and mental impact is pretty much the same, whether it is cancer of the breast, the cervix, the liver, the stomach, the lung, or a brain tumour.

The Centre accepts that, so far as cancer doctors are concerned, there is a great deal of difference between the various types of cancer but, in every case, your body has gone horribly out of control. No matter what type of cancer you have, the stress and anxiety which results from having the feeling that there is a nasty time-bomb ticking away inside you, will be the same.

What has happened at Bristol since the trauma of the Chilvers report is that the Centre has taken a long hard look at what is on offer, and this has given an opportunity to modify and alter and rearrange the approach. The diet, for which Bristol has become particularly famous, basically still stands, and there has seemed no need to change it radically.

Evidence which has emerged during the years since Dr Alec Forbes first formulated the diet has strengthened, rather than weakened, Bristol's initial hunch that this was an anti-cancer and anti-tumour diet which could certainly help the body to detoxify itself.

Bristol believes that the original intention of being basically a spiritual healing centre was the right one, and that spiritual healing provides the basis of all genuine healing. When the spirit, the emotions, the non-physical aspects, are healed, then the body often follows suit. The new science of psychoneuroimmunology – usually known as PNI – underlines the important links between mind, body and spirit.

Spiritual healers believe that all physical illness is basically a dis-ease within, a being out of touch with the spirit, something stumbled upon by Prince Charles, who opened the Centre, in his "alternative medicine" days. When you heal the spirit, you can often heal the mind. Even the most orthodox doctors are now accepting that the mind may play a far larger part than previously recognised in the development of serious illness.

At any rate, the staff at Bristol have seen enough dramatic improvement through spiritual healing to confirm the early belief that this was central to the healing of a disease as terrifying as cancer. It is also clear though that, unless the Centre expands to become the size of a general hospital, it will never be able to take in as residents all the cancer patients who may want to come. As it looks unlikely, at least in the foreseeable future, that "Bristol" residential centres will open in other parts of the country, the best that can be done in this regard is to promote Bristol's approach through educational courses and present a rationale for the holistic aproach into environments where people with cancer receive their primary care.

The Centre is also holding "life revival" weekends for those who are not exactly ill, but who feel jaded and in need of nurturing themselves back to genuine health. Although these weekends are aimed mainly at health professionals, there is no limit on who can attend. Why wait to be ill to benefit from this self-help approach?

Doctors, nurses and other medical personnel are becoming ever more interested in psychological approaches to cancer, and this is bringing the new science of psycho-oncology into being. For although cancer research is still proceeding at an expensive and ever-growing rate, in our view there will never be a cancer "cure" until the psychological implications are properly understood.

Pat Pilkington, who is now at the head of the Bristol team explains what she sees as the Centre's new role in the nineties and beyond:

We are here to remind people of who they are. At first, some people may wonder what our programme has to do with cancer, when they see such things as art therapy, music therapy, massage and circle dancing on the brochure.

But the point of all our therapies is to remind people that they are, above all, spiritual beings. We help patients to raise their consciousness and awareness so that they can move forward with a new confidence in themselves. That is why, when the Chilvers report came out, we were so surprised to learn that we were seen as competition by the orthodox people. We have always seen ourselves as having a quite different role from conventional cancer doctors and specialists. It is true that the shock of the Chilvers backlash numbed us, and it took a long time for its severity to sink in. We eventually realised that we were in great peril, but we still thought that it would merely be a blip and that soon people would forget and we could return to normal.

We learned, on taking expert advice, that we had allowed ourselves to be very isolated and that we had not liaised enough with the orthodox world or with other cancer charities. We had kept ourselves to ourselves and, as such, could be accused of arrogance.

Of course, we had never intended to be arrogant – we were just helping cancer patients in the way that seemed best, and while they flocked to us, there was no need to change our ways. Everybody came to us – we never had to advertise, or to seek for patients. We had more enquiries than we could comfortably deal with and we were always full.

But as a result of the Chilvers report, we decided to have a more "open door" approach. We have now made strong links with the epidemiology department at Bristol University, and our courses are now accredited by a recognised university.

We have also realised the importance of having a strong nutritional database which collates evidence and research on nutrition from everywhere in the world. We now have our food checked by professional nutritionists, and this came in after we were accused of killing people following the Chilvers report.

Chilvers turned us in our tracks, and we now believe it has been a blessing in disguise. We were all seriously overworked, and we believed we could take on everything. But although we are now forging strong links with the wider cancer community, we have not changed our basic approach, which is to provide a transformational experience for people with cancer.

We are also looking seriously at PNI, to try and discover the specific ways in which the mind affects the body, and how brain chemicals transmit themselves to other parts of the system, for good or ill.

Orthodox cancer researchers are now excitedly looking at the genetic implications of cancer, of the importance of the family history. This has been hailed as a major step forward but, so far, there is little that can be offered once you know you are at risk because of your family history.

Cancer specialists now know that women who have a history of breast cancer in their family have a vastly increased risk of developing it themselves, but so far the only "treatment" available is to have a bilateral mastectomy, the removal of healthy breasts – just in case.

Some women have agreed to this terrible treatment, but of course, it won't necessarily prevent cancer spreading elsewhere, and the greatest problem of all with cancer is that secondaries can form in other parts of the body, often in far-distant sites and in places where it may not be possible to remove the offending organ.

So far as Bristol is concerned, "prophylactic" surgery of this type is not a genuine treatment. We are far more interested in the growth of psycho-oncology, which takes on board the far-reaching psychological implications of cancer.

Cancer treatment and approaches have led the way, and nowhere else in medicine is there such an acceptance of the part that the mind and spirit can play in the development of the disease. Cancer specialists have accepted that cancer is as much a psychological as a physical disease, because they've had to. This realisation has been forced on them simply because cancer has beaten, and continues to beat, all the treatments that they have been able to offer.

In his book, *An Introduction to Psycho-Oncology*, translated into English by Heather Goodare, Swiss psychiatrist Patrice Guex explains how he sees the psychological aspects of cancer. As Professor Karol Sikora says in his foreword, these have been ignored for far too long.

It is time to take on board the overwhelming truth that we do not realise just how alone we are until cancer strikes. Before, we might have imagined we had a loving family, that we were supported and nurtured by our parents, partners, children, friends and colleagues. When cancer strikes, this is often seen to be an illusion – all the "support" instantly falls away, and we realise that we have built a house of cards, without a firm foundation, and that we have been living in a fools' paradise.

The truth is, of course, that we are all ultimately alone. Nobody can take away our pain, nobody can go through our treatment for us, and those nearest and dearest may not be strong enough to offer support. By contrast, they may have completely depended on us.

This comes out time and again at Bristol residents' weeks, when cancer patients discover that they are expected to support their relatives through the treatment, rather than the other way round. Husbands, wives and children can suddenly completely collapse when they learn of the cancer. The sense of isolation is the most overwhelming emotion experienced by cancer patients. Because of this, it seems to make sense that support groups, or in technical language "good-quality affective bonds", are an essential factor in helping patients to cope. In extreme situations, we bond best with those who are going through a similar trauma, as they are often the only people who can actually understand what it is like.

Psycho-oncologists now acknowledge that support groups can be helpful for people coping with cancer – a message which, we believe, some have learned from Bristol, where cancer patients have always supported each other.

The main fears on diagnosis, Dr Guex believes, are these: fear of alienation and isolation; fear of mutilation; the sudden confrontation with one's own vulnerability, and fear of loss of control.

In order to cope with cancer, the patient has to be able to face up to the disease itself, the treatments, to come to terms with the possibly dramatic alterations in his or her life, and to develop good relationships with the medical team. For this, help may be needed.

The ambiguity of cancer, says Dr Guex, is that it is experienced as life-threatening but is treated as a chronic sickbed. This means that any patient's adaptation to the disease must be a complex process of searching for meaning in life. On diagnosis, people often ask themselves for the first time: why am I here? Where am I going? Where did I come from? Spiritual questions often force themselves to the front of the mind for the very first time ever, in much the same way that even professed atheists may pray to God when their lives are in imminent danger.

In the past, there was no place for cancer patients to be able to grapple with these questions. Bristol has always provided a spiritual milieu where it is safe to discuss these matters.

At Bristol, great emphasis has always been placed on the quality of life. Because of this, death is not seen as a failure as, after all, we all have to die, and for some people it might even come as a blessed release. For this reason, Bristol is not pinning its hopes on a cure. But even terminally ill people can improve the quality of their lives for the time they may have left. And nobody knows for sure how long this will be. Very many patients who have gone to Bristol having been given only weeks, or months to live are still alive many years later. But not all. Bristol cannot provide miracle cures – but they can give hope.

The worst thing is to try to live without hope.

Psycho-oncology has taken on board many of the concepts which have been well known at Bristol for very many years. We have always accepted that the impact of cancer does not affect only the patient, but family and close friends as well. They may be even more upset than the patient, as they fear losing a loved one any minute. Also, most relatives are not themselves cancer experts and they feel helpless in the face of such a serious disease. This adds to their stress and discomfort, and possibly panic.

Mostly, relatives don't know how to help the patient and, very often, discussion of the illness is not encouraged.

Although at Bristol they treat all cancers as the same disease, they also recognise that reaction to the diagnosis is a very individual thing. Some patients feel that having cancer is at least partly compensated for by the positive aspects of increased self-awareness, raised consciousness and a new assertiveness. For others, the experience is a terrible trauma which is hard, maybe even impossible, to accept.

It also has to be understood that cancer affects one's sexual and emotional life and intimate relationships. So at Bristol, people are encouraged to talk about their sexual lives before and since cancer, if they want to. Again, this is something they may hesitate to mention to their oncologists. But if it preys on the mind, it is important, and sexuality is so central to the lives of the majority of people, men and women, that it cannot just be dismissed as something trivial.

This is also something now being accepted as valid by psycho-oncologists. Very many breast and cervical cancer patients talk of their fears that they will no longer have a sex life, no longer be considered attractive by their partners or lovers, and their fears that they will certainly not be able to have any new relationships.

Because, as the prevailing attitude to massage shows us, patients often see themselves as ill and unattractive, they may not be receiving the physical warmth and comfort which might make all the difference. Feeling themselves to be unattractive and unlovable, they isolate themselves even more. Dr Guex believes that libido summons up "vital energy" so its expression should be encouraged.

This is controversial, as there have so far been few studies on the sexuality of cancer patients.

It is known that some cancer treatments definitely lower or remove libido, while others increase it. But so far, we don't know what effect these treatments may have on the psyche. It's something which people are often reluctant to talk about, as many cancer patients imagine they must be grateful for anything which might zap the tumour, and never mind the price that may have to be paid in other areas of their lives.

Psycho-oncologists accept that few diseases, if any, provoke as much anxiety as cancer, and that anxiety is at its height when treatment is broken off, or finished and the patient is left without a support system.

In the past, this is often when people have come to Bristol; we now hope that, through coming at an earlier stage, suitable support networks can be set up so that this feeling of isolation and panic, of having nobody to talk to after treatment has been apparently concluded, will become a distant memory.

We now know that up to forty-five per cent of cancer patients try complementary therapies at some stage of their cancer journey. Evidence from psycho-oncology studies has also confirmed that when health is seriously under attack, patients need affection, approval and security – all things that Bristol from its earliest days had tried to provide.

On patient support groups, which we are particularly enthusiastic about, Dr Guex observes that patients do not find it depressing to meet other people who have been through the same tragic experiences.

The existence of the group, he believes, allows us to recognise the universality of the questions that are asked, and the reactions that come about. It is extremely comforting to know that, however silly, trivial or ignorant your question may seem, there are others in the room who have wondered exactly the same things. But, like you, they may have hesitated in the past to voice their query or complaint.

American cancer surgeon Dr Bernie Siegel, author of *Peace, Love and Healing* and *Love, Medicine and Miracles*, is greatly beloved by many current and former Bristol patients. His view is that a serious disease can be a gift, a potent agent of transformation. For some people, he says, the challenge of illness actually gives their life a purpose.

We are always liable to stay well and healthy, he says, when we have a sense of real purpose in our lives, and orthodox physicians remain all too rarely aware of this.

He also says, commenting on complementary therapies, that what suits one person will be anathema to another – something which has always been held to be the case at Bristol. The Bristol message will never be pushed down everybody's throat, and cancer patients who prefer to stick with orthodox treatments must be allowed to make that choice.

The messages that are coming out from enlightened cancer specialists worldwide are those which back up the approach which has always been taken at Bristol: with something as problematic as cancer, there will probably never be a simple pill or operation which will eradicate the tumour without causing side-effects to the rest of the system.

Cancer is now widely accepted as having a dramatic psychological impact, so it seems sensible to tackle the mental and emotional implications, rather than pretending they don't, or at least, shouldn't, exist. Very often, the "placebo effect" is spoken of disparagingly, as if it is of little account. Yet, increasingly doctors are coming to accept that the placebo effect is one of the most effective healing phenomena of all.

Why do new drugs always seem so much more effective than the old ones? Not necessarily because they *are* more effective, but simply because as they are new, only just on the market, they give renewed hope and promise. It is also noticeable how very often the power of new drugs to heal is temporary: after they have been around for a few years, they no longer seem quite so good.

Bernie Siegel says that we must accept that we can't cure everything, and that we should not see death as a failure, as it will come to us all anyway in the end.

At Bristol, it is not always possible to help people to carry on living, but at the very least, they can be helped to experience a peaceful death, knowing that healing can occur on many different levels.

The struggles of the Bristol Centre to survive since the impact of the Chilvers report, and the body blow it dealt not just to Bristol but to complementary therapies generally, have shown that there is no room for complacency and the Centre must keep monitoring its approach to see whether it is still valid, whether it needs to be modified, what new concepts need to be taken on board.

Bristol's message has now been taken out into the community, and much of it has become accepted. The once-fringe activities are becoming ever more mainstream. The hope is that the Bristol Centre will continue to offer the very best that is available in complementary care and valid help for cancer patients and to enable those who cannot come to Bristol themselves to take advantage of the holistic approach.

Bristol gives cancer patients the chance to turn a crisis into an opportunity, to look at their lives, their relationships, their sense of themselves and to learn to sing their own song.

That has always been the underlying message and purpose of the Bristol Cancer Help Centre, and we expect it always will be.

Glossary

Acupuncture Ancient Chinese therapy which uses very fine needles to stimulate energies on points of the body, known as meridians.

Alternative treatments Branches of medicine not currently espoused by "orthodox" medical science.

Biopsy Removal and examination of a small piece of tissue from the living body to test for possible malignancy.

Cancer A disease whereby body cells grow in an uncontrolled way.

Carcinogen Any substance known, or thought, to cause cancer in humans or animals.

Carcinoma A malignant tumour which arises from body cells that line surfaces of the body, such as the skin, the intestines, the respiratory tract.

Cervical smear A method of taking a small sample of cells from the cervix and examining them under the microscope for possible cancerous changes. Also known as a Pap smear.

Cervix The entrance to the womb.

Chemotherapy Treatment of cancer by using combinations of chemicals to kill the cancerous cells.

Colposcopy The use of a flexible instrument to examine the neck of the womb with a magnifying glass.

Complementary medicine All the "alternative" forms of medicine practised with the emphasis on cooperation with and support from the orthodox forms of medicine.

Controlled clinical trial Comparison of the results of a particular treatment in patients who received the treatment with those who did not.

Holistic treatment Forms of treatment which take the whole person – mind, body and spirit – into account. Not to be confused with alternative or complementary treatments.

Homoeopathy An old-established system of medicine which uses tiny doses of active substances to promote healing of mind, body and spirit. Homoeopathic remedies usually have no adverse side-effects.

Hospice A hospital or centre specially equipped for the care of dying patients.

Hysterectomy Removal of the womb by surgery.

Immune system The body system which recognises and kills foreign and invading cells.

Leukaemia Cancer occurring in the blood-forming tissue of the bone marrow or lymph nodes.

Lumpectomy Removal of cancerous breast lump (rather than whole breast).

Lymph Fluid circulating in the lymphatic vessels.

Lymphatic system A system similar to the blood system, which carries away toxic matter from body cells, and through which lymph circulates.

Macrobiotic A dietary system based on the Chinese system of yin and yang, providing a balanced, toxic-free diet. Often used in the alternative treatment of cancer.

Malignant Any tumour which has become invasive.

Mammogram An X-ray technique used for detecting lumps in the breast which are impossible to feel manually, or to see with the naked eye.

Mastectomy Surgical treatment for cancer where most or all of the breast is removed.

Melanoma A type of cancer which develops from the cells in the skin which carry melanin pigment.

Metastasis The spread of an original cancer to other parts of the body.

Oestrogen Hormone produced mainly by the ovaries in women.

Oncogenes "Cancer genes". These may facilitate the spread of cancer when they mutate.

Oncologist Cancer specialist.

Oncology The specialist study of cancer and its treatments.

Organic produce Food that is produced without the use of chemicals, ie: pesticides, fertilisers and herbicides.

Orthodox Mainstream medical science, founded in a Cartesian or mechanistic view of the human being, whose principal therapeutic techniques are allopathic drug therapy and surgery.

Prosthesis Artificial substitute for a missing part.

Psychoneuroimmunology The study of relationships between the mind, nervous system and immune system in cancer.

Psycho-oncology Study of the psychological aspects of cancer.

Psychosomatic medicine The study of the relationship between the mind and body in illness.

Radiotherapy Use of X-rays to treat tumours. Also known as radiation therapy.

Remission A state in which the cancer appears to be inactive.

Secondaries Tumours which have spread (metastasized) to distant sites; not the primary cancer site.

Spontaneous remission A state whereby the cancer appears to have receded of its own accord.

Tamoxifen A chemical compound used to treat breast cancer by interfering with the ability of oestrogen to get into breast cancer cells.

Terminally ill From terminal, meaning final, or the end.

Tumour Another word for cancerous cells.

Ultrasound A technique using sound waves for generating images of organs in the body.

White blood cells An important part of the immune system made by cells in the bone marrow.

Veganism Diets which exclude all animal produce, including dairy produce, eggs and honey.

Useful Addresses

When the **Bristol Cancer Help Centre** first began in 1980, there were very few organisations, complementary therapies or practitioners. However, the situation today is very different. In the intervening years, there has been a mushrooming of different therapies, and those at the beginning of their cancer journey are faced with what can seem like a maze of different options. It can be very confusing, especially as complementary therapies are very personal: different things appeal to different people, and it can take time to find out what seems right. With this in mind, we have listed the major organisations (marked with an **) who will provide details of bona fide practitioners and up-to-date information on: Counselling, Massage, Homoeopathy, Herbal Medicine, Reflexology, Aromatherapy, Shiatsu, Psychotherapy, Acupuncture, Hypnotherapy, Osteopathy, Naturopathy, Chinese Medicine and Alexander Technique. These "umbrella" organisations exist to maintain standards of practice and to protect those seeking their services.

The national cancer organisations and complementary therapies mentioned in this book which are not covered by the major bodies are listed separately.

Where possible, each organisation has a short paragraph giving basic information about the services it provides. We hope this will be a starting point for obtaining further information. Most of the organisations listed here will require an SAE.

Bristol Cancer Help Centre (BCHC)
Grove House, Cornwallis Grove
Clifton, Bristol 1BS8 4PG
Tel: 0117 974 3216 (9am–5pm)

Please contact reception for details of courses, educational programmes, workshops and seminars. The BCHC also offers telephone counselling and advice, a doctor's phone-in service, healing, individual complementary therapies, information on a wide range of therapies, contacts for support groups and therapists, conference and workshop facilities, books, tapes and videos.

"Umbrella" Organisations

Council for Complementary and Alternative Medicine (CCAM)**
179 Gloucester Place
London NW1 6DX
Tel: 0171 724 9103 Fax: 0171 724 5330

Formed in 1984 the CCAM provides a forum for communication and cooperation between professional bodies representing acupuncture, herbal medicine, homoeopathy, naturopathy and osteopathy. It promotes the highest standards of training, qualifications and treatment in complementary medicine and aims to make this as accessible as possible to the public. All practitioners of the professional bodies represented by the CCAM have undergone a minimum of three years' training in their chosen therapy, and are bound by strict codes of conduct. The CCAM will put you in touch with its relevant bodies.

The Institute for Complementary Medicine (ICM)**
PO Box 194
London SE16 1QZ
Tel: 0171 237 5165 Fax: 0171 237 5175

Founded as an independent charity in 1982, the ICM works to ensure the public safe access to reliable complementary practitioners and a source of unbiased information about training and treatment. The Institute administers the British Register of Complementary Practitioners, which has 17 divisions covering Aromatherapy, Chinese Medicine, Colour Therapy, Counselling, Energy Medicine, Healer Counselling, Homoeopathy, Hypnotherapy, Massage, Nutrition, Osteopathy and Reflexology.

The ICM also sponsors research into natural treatments, education and training, publishes a journal, and has a library of books, journals and research documents for public, media and official use.

The British Complementary Medicine Association (BCMA)**
St Charles' Hospital
94 Exmoor Street
London W10 6DZ
Tel: 0181 964 1205 Fax: 0171 964 1207

A Union of Associations of Complementary Medicine which represents the interests of therapies at all levels, and protects the rights of both the public and practitioners. It also aims to raise standards and promote complementary medicine within an integrated health care system. The BCMA will provide information and advice.

The British Holistic Medical Association (BHMA)**
179 Gloucester Place
London NW1 6DX
Tel: 0171 262 5299 (12.30pm – 6.30pm Tuesdays)

The BHMA aims to educate doctors and health care professionals, encouraging them to treat patients as individuals using the "holistic" approach. It publishes a quarterly newsletter for its members, and can provide self-help books and tapes. A publications list is available.

The Research Council for Complementary Medicine (RCCM)
60 Great Ormond Street
London WC1 3JF
Tel: 0171 833 8897 Fax: 0171 278 7412

Founded in 1983, the RCCM is a charity which aims to promote rigorous scientific research into all aspects of complementary medicine, and to see that the results are widely distributed and translated into effective medical practice.

National Cancer Organisations

BACUP
3 Bath Place
Rivington Street
London EC2A 3JR
Tel: 0171 613 2121

Information Service (Mon – Thurs 10am – 7pm: Fri 10am – 5.30pm):
Freephone 0800 181199
Counselling Service (Mon – Fri 10am – 5.30pm): 0171 696 9000
Administration: 0171 696 9003

Cancer nurses provide one-to-one information and emotional support for patients, relatives and friends. You can either call or write to the Information Service. The one-to-one Counselling Service offers weekly appointments for up to eight sessions based at BACUP's London office. Over 40 publications on different types of cancer are available, including treatments, and the practical and emotional issues faced by people with cancer. All of BACUP's services are free and confidential. A list of national support groups is also available.

CancerLink
17 Britannia Street
London WC1X 9JN

Groups and Supporters (9.30am – 5.30pm) Tel: 0171 833 2818
Information service (9.30am – 5.30pm) Tel: 0171 833 2451
Asian Language Line (Mon & Fri 10am – 12.30pm) Tel: 0171 713 7867
Information Service (Edinburgh 9.30am – 5pm) Tel: 0131 228 5557
MACline (Young people): Freephone 0800 591028 Mon – Fri 9.30am – 5pm

CancerLink provides emotional support and information on all aspects of cancer, and assistance and training for cancer self-help and support groups. It will help set up new groups, and put people in touch with individuals through the Black Network and one-to-one register. CancerLink also issues a wide range of publications (including *Link-up*, a quarterly magazine), and provides support for individuals wishing to support others on a one-to-one basis, which can be particularly relevant for those living in isolated areas, or who have an unusual cancer or treatment, or where additional factors are important such as ethnic origin, language, sexuality or personal circumstances. CancerLink has a special awareness of minority groups.

Other Organisations and Therapies

Anthroposophical Medical Association *(for information on Iscador)*
Weleda (UK) Ltd
Heanor Road
Ilkeston
Derbyshire DE7 8DR
Tel: 01602 303151 Fax: 01602 440349

Iscador is one of the many well-established treatments offered by Anthroposophical Medicine, founded by Dr Rudolf Steiner: other treatments include herbal medicines, massage, nutrition, movement and artistic therapy. Iscador is manufactured by Weleda, and it is normal for someone requiring Iscador treatment to have a course supervised by an Anthroposophical or homoeopathic doctor. Information about Anthroposophical Medicine and a register of practitioners can be obtained from Rudolf Steiner House, 35 Park Road, London NW1 Tel: 0171 723 4400.

Bach Flower Remedies
Dr Edward Bach Centre
Mount Vernon
Sotwell, Wallingford
Oxon OX10 0PZ
Tel (general information): 01491 839489
Tel (advice, treatment & information): 01491 834678

Founded in 1936, these long-established and well-known herbal preparations are widely available throughout the UK. The Centre will provide information booklets about different essences, advice and information as well as a register of local practitioners.

Dancing Circles
Wesley Cottage
New Road, East Huntspill
High Bridge, Somerset TA9 3PT
Tel: 01278 786307

This number will put you in contact with the editors of *Grapevine*, a quarterly publication giving information on circle dance tapes, booklets and instructors. It will also provide lists of teachers and classes.

Issels-Institut Für Ganzheitsmedizin GmbH
Maria-Viktoria-Str. 22
D-7570 Baden-Baden
Germany

Founded in 1951 by Dr Josef Issels MD, it was the first European hospital for the treatment of incurable cancer patients (i.e.: those beyond conventional help).

MusicSpace Trust
Southville Centre
Bristol BS3 1QG
Tel: 0117 963 8000 Fax: 0117 966 9889

The Trust, opened in 1991, aims to set up a network of nationwide centres to provide community-based music therapy services for both individuals and groups with wide-ranging mental and physical health care needs. Also provides training in conjunction with Bristol University.

National Federation of Spiritual Healers (NFSH)
Old Manor Farm Studio
Church Street
Sunbury on Thames
Middlesex TW16 6RG
Tel: 01932 783164 Fax: 01932 779648
Healer referral service: 01791 616080 (Mon – Fri: 9.00am – 5.00pm)

A charity founded in 1955, the NFSH is a recognised body of spiritual healers who have undergone the Federation's training. They will provide details of healers in your area as well as advice and information. They also have centres in other parts of the UK.

Soil Association
86 Colston Street
Bristol BS1 5BB
Tel: 0272 290661

The Association will provide information on the following: organic growing (both domestic and commercial): where to buy organic food; different pesticides and their effects; and farming.

The British Association of Art Therapists (BAAT)
11a Richmond Road
Brighton
Sussex BN2 3RL
(There is no telephone number. Please send a letter and SAE)

Provides information about the use and practice of art therapy, training courses, and a register of practising art therapists.

The Gerson Therapy
The Gerson Institute
PO Box 430
Bonita
California 92002 USA

The Institute will provide up-to-date information on British contacts, and details about the Gerson diet.

Vegan Society
7 Battle Road,
St Leonards-on-Sea
East Sussex TN37 7AA
Tel: 01424 427393 Fax: 01424 717064

Founded in 1944, this registered charity will provide an information pack, including details of the society, nutritional information and leaflets. Advice is also available over the phone.

Vegetarian Society
Park Dale
Dunham, Altrincham
Cheshire WA14 4QG
Tel: 0161 928 0793

A charity founded in 1847, they will provide a free information pack with recipes, available resources and leaflets. Membership is available, and they publish a magazine called *The Vegetarian*.

White Eagle Lodge
New Lands, Brewells Lane
Rake, Liss
Hampshire GU33 7HY
Tel: 01730 893300 Fax: 01730 892235

Founded in 1936, this charitable organisation is a well-established, recognised body of healers with a worldwide register. They will provide information, advice, training (for members), and a list of practitioners in or near your area. They also hold healing services every week.

Meditation, Relaxation, Breathing and Visualisation

No general organisations can be given here, as meditation, relaxation, breathing and visualisation tend to be developed more on an individual basis, or through specific groups or practices. Breathing, relaxation and meditation have long been associated with traditional Eastern disciplines such as Yoga and Transcendental Meditation (in the Bibliography you will find some publications about how to develop and apply these for yourself). The Bristol Cancer Help Centre will also be able to provide contact numbers for Yoga and different schools of meditation, or you may find that there are meditation or prayer groups in your area. Check with your local library or church.

Children and Cancer

There is a belief at the Bristol Cancer Help Centre that children diagnosed with cancer require very special treatment that cannot be provided at the Centre at present. Those with children affected by cancer are well served with many specialist organisations and centres, who provide not only excellent care but also practical and emotional support for parents. The following two organisations will provide a starting point for information and advice, or refer you to others who can help with your particular situation:

Childhood Cancer and Leukaemia Link (CALL)
36 Knowles Avenue
Crowthorne
Berkshire RG11 6DU
Tel: 01344 750319

CALL links families in a similar area or situation whose child has had cancer or leukaemia. Publishes a quarterly newsletter, provides information and advice.

Rainbow Centre For Children With Cancer And Life-Threatening Illness
PO Box 604
Bristol
Avon BS99 1SW
Tel: 0117 973 0752/973 6228 (24-hour answerphone)

This is a support centre for children with cancer or other life-threatening illness and their families. They offer counselling, healing, meditation, diet and psychological support. Bereavement counselling is also available. Families are seen free of charge.

Practical Help

There are many organisations which provide hands-on care and nursing for those with cancer, or help and support for those looking after people with cancer. Usually you will be able to access local help via these organisations:

Cancer Relief Macmillan Fund (CRMF)
Anchor House
15–19 Britten Street
London SW3 3TZ
Tel: 0171 351 7811 Fax: 0171 376 8098

The CRMF is a national charity devoted to caring for people with cancer. At the heart of their work are the Macmillan nurses, of whom there are now more than 1,000. They have also established a whole network of cancer care throughout the UK, including specialist care centres, grants for patients in financial need, Macmillan doctors, and a nursing and medical education programme. In addition, they offer information direct to patients and families through four associated charities.

Carers National Association
20/25 Glasshouse Yard
London EC1A 4JS
Tel: 0171 490 8818
Tel (carers line): 0171 490 8898 (Mon – Fri: 1pm – 4 pm)

National organisation providing advice, information and support for relatives, the chronically ill or disabled, and giving practical advice plus contacts for local self-help groups. The organisation has other headquarters in different regions.

Hospice Information Service
St Christopher's Hospice
51–59 Lawrie Park Road
Sydenham
London SE26 6DZ
Tel: 0181 778 9252 (Mon – Fri 9am – 9pm)

A national resource link for those seeking information on hospice care, practical help and pain control. They will provide a directory of hospices throughout the UK and overseas (please send an SAE), and are able to offer information, support and advice.

Self-Help and Support Groups

These are covered by CancerLink and BACUP, who can provide up-to-date, comprehensive information on all aspects of support groups and self-help. This includes helping to set up a new group, advice, local contacts, education and training. CancerLink provides a yearly updated directory of Cancer support and self-help groups (*see page 136*).

NHS Hospitals Offering Complementary and Holistic Therapies

Increasing demand for complementary approaches to cancer, together with a growing understanding by orthodox medicine of their value, means that more NHS establishments are beginning to incorporate some popular therapies into their services. The more common therapies offered are: counselling, reflexology, healing, osteopathy, aromatherapy and massage. Obviously each hospital will be different, depending on the area and resources available. The simplest way to find out what your local NHS services offer is to contact them directly.

Bibliography

The number of publications available on cancer-related subjects is vast, with new books coming out every year. We have selected titles covering most subjects mentioned in the book and which we have found to be of most benefit to a wide range of people. Some of these may be out of print, but should be obtainable through a well-stocked library. Several of the titles are available from the Bristol Cancer Help Centre. Please send an SAE for the book and tape list.

Anthroposophical Medicine: V. Bott (Rudolf Steiner Press 1982)

The Bristol De-Tox Diet for Cancer Patients: A. Forbes (Keats 1986)

The Bristol Programme: P. Brohn (Century 1987) – out of print

The Calm Technique: P. Wilson (Thorsons 1991)

Cancer and Nutrition: Dr R. Daniel & Dr S. Goodman (*available only from the Bristol Cancer Help Centre* 1994)

Cancer as a Turning Point: Dr L. LeShan (Gateway 1989)

Cancer Information At Your Fingertips: V. Speechley and M. Rosenfield (Class Publishing 1992)

A Cancer Therapy – The Results of 50 Cases: M. Gerson (Totality Books, Del Mar 1990)

Complete Book of Massage: C. M. Hudson (Dorling Kindersey 1988)

Coping Successfully with Pain: N. Shone (Sheldon 1992)

Creative Visualisation: S. Gawain (Bantam 1985)

Dictionary of Bach Flower Remedies: T. Hyne-Jones (C.W. Daniel 1987)

Dirty Medicine: M. Walker (Slingshot 1993)

The Everyday Meditator: Osho (Boxtree 1993)

Gentle Giants: P. Brohn (Century 1986) – out of print

A Gentle Way with Cancer: B. Kidman (Century 1983)

Getting Well Again: C. Simonton (Bantam Books, USA 1991)

The Good Retreat Guide: S. Whiteaker (Rider 1991)

Heal Cancer: R. Cilento (Hill of Content, Melbourne 1993)

Heal Thyself: E. Bach (C. W. Publishers 1988)

Healing Into Life and Death: S. Levine (Gateway 1987)

How to Meditate: Dr L. LeShan (Aquarian 1993)

An Introduction to Psycho-Oncology: P. Guex (trans. H. Goodare) (Routledge 1993)

Laughter – The Best Medicine: R. Holden (Thorsons 1993)

Living Beyond Limits: D. Spiegel (Vermilion 1994)
Living, Loving and Healing: B. Siegel (Aquarian 1993)
Living with Death and Dying: E. Kübler-Ross (Souvenir Press 1981)
Love, Medicine and Miracles: B. Siegel (Aquarian 1986)
Loving Medicine: R. Thomson (Gateway 1989)
Maximum Immunity: M. A. Weiner (Gateway 1986)
Moon over the Water: J. Macbeth (Gateway Books)
Music Therapy: An Art Beyond Words: L. Bunt (Routledge 1994)
Nutritional Medicine: Davies and Stewart (Pan 1987)
Peace, Love and Healing: B. Siegel (Aquarian 1990)
Personal Growth Handbook: L. Hodgkinson (Piatkus Books 1993)
Quantum Healing: D. Chopra (Bantam 1989)
Raw Energy: L. Kenton (Vermilion, 1994)
The Road Less Travelled: M. Scott Peck, (Arrow Rider 1988)
Self-Massage: Young (Thorsons 1992)
Spiritual Healing: L. Hodgkinson (Piatkus 1992)
Sun Over Mountain: J. Macbeth (Gateway Books)
Teach Yourself to Meditate: E. Harrison (Thorsons 1993)
Third Opinion: *An International Directory to Alternative Therapy Centres for the Treatment and Prevention of Cancer*: J. M. Fink (Avery Publishing 1988)
365+1 Vegan Recipes: L. Leneman (Thorsons 1993)
A Time to Heal: B. Bishop (New English Library 1989)
Unconditional Life: D. Chopra (Bantam 1991)
Who Dies?: S. Levine (Anchor 1982)
You Can Conquer Cancer: I. Gawler (1987)

Index

absent healing, 118
acupuncture, 22, 90
adrenaline, 80, 111, 112
affirmations, 78
alcohol, 14, 60, 61, 68
Alcoholics Anonymous, 100
Alexander Technique, 83–4, 85
anger, 113–14
animal protein, 64
art therapy, 16–17, 20, 97–8, 99, 119
arthritis, 91
asthma, 84
attitudes to cancer, 78–9
autogenic training, 85

Bagenal, F.S., 33
Bailey, Thea, 91
BBC, 28, 29, 32
beta-carotene, 68
Bishop, Beata, 120
Board, Lillian, 23
Bodmer, Sir Walter, 29–31, 38–9
Bourke, Isla, 38–9, 41
bowel cancer, 61, 66
Brahma Kumaris, 111–12
brain, meditation, 111
breast cancer, 22–3, 33–5, 88, 89, 100, 126, 128
breasts, massage, 89
breathing, 9, 19, 80–6
Bristol Cancer Help Centre:
    residents' weeks, 3–20, 126
    early history, 21–31

Chilvers report, 32–42, 50–3, 122, 124, 125, 129
    after the Chilvers report, 43–5, 52–4
    Patients' and Supporters' Panel, 45, 103
    future developments, 122–30
Bristol Diet, 6, 13–14, 27, 59–69, 124
    Chilvers report, 33–4
    low fat, 65
    low protein, 64
    natural food, 65
    raw food, 65–6
    recipes, 70–3
    salt, 66
    stimulants, 67–8
    sugar, 67
    vitamin and mineral supplements, 9, 68–9
Bristol Study see Chilvers report
Bristol Survey Support Group (BSSG), 38–9, 41, 43, 45, 51, 122
Bristol University, 125
British Medical Journal, 42, 64
Brohn, Penny, 12, 14, 16, 21, 22–7, 29, 31, 32, 40, 41, 49–50, 52, 57, 61, 65, 76–7, 83, 110, 120
Brookman, Ute, 13–14

caffeine, 7, 14, 60, 67
'cancer personality', 9–10
Cancer Positive (television programme), 38
Cancer Research Campaign (CRC), 31, 34, 38–9
CancerLink, 100–1, 103, 104

carers, 17
carrot and lentil soup, 71
cashew nuts:
    parsnip and cashew bake, 72
cervical cancer, 45, 47–9, 128
Channel Four, 38
chanting, 111
Charing Cross Hospital, 87–8
Charity Commission, 38, 39, 50
Charles, Prince of Wales, 28, 124
Chelsea Pastoral Foundation, 106
chemotherapy, 15, 59
chickpeas:
    hummus, 70–1
Chilvers, Professor Clair, 33, 34,
    36, 37
Chilvers report, 33–42, 50–3, 122,
    124, 125, 129
chocolate, 67
Church of England, 116
circle dancing, 91–3
coffee, 6–7, 60, 61, 67–8
coffee enemas, 60
Conley, Rosemary, 65
counselling, 10, 27, 104–8
crumble, fruit, 73

Daily Telegraph, 50
dairy produce, 9, 65
dancing, circle, 91–3
Daniel, Dr Rosy, 31, 121–2
Dean, Michael, 29
death, desire for, 79
detoxification therapy, 60
diabetes, 64, 84, 91
diaries, 98–9
diet see Bristol Diet
drugs, 129

Easton, D.F., 33
'effort syndrome', 84
emotions:
    buried, 113
    coping with negative, 9
    impact of illness, 44
    music and, 94
    releasing buried, 85–6, 106

empowerment, 14
enemas, coffee, 60
energy:
    shiatsu, 90–1
    spiritual healing, 117
Evening Standard, 34

families, 105, 126, 127
fat, low-fat diet, 65
fear, 7–8, 17–18, 57, 80, 82, 86,
    127
feelings see emotions
fish, 64
Forbes, Dr Alec, 6, 25–7, 29, 31,
    57, 60, 61, 63–4, 124
Fox, Robin, 42
free radicals, 68
friends, 105, 127
fruit, 60
fruit crumble, 73

gall bladder, 60
genetic factors, 125–6
A Gentle Way with Cancer?, 28,
    29–31
Gerson, Dr Max, 60–1, 66
Gerson clinic, 25, 36, 120
Goodare, Heather, 38–9, 41
group work, 100–4, 126–7, 128
growth hormones, 65
Guex, Dr Patrice, 126, 127, 128
guilt, 11
Guy Pilkington Foundation, 28

Hammersmith Hospital, 35–6, 40,
    53, 90
Harris, E., 33
Harris, Dr Myles, 34
Harrison, Eric, 112, 113, 114–5
Hastings Cancer Help Centre, 50
healing, 14–15, 80, 112–13, 114–
    15
    spiritual healing, 16, 21, 116–18
HealthWatch, 37
heart disease, 64, 87–8
high blood pressure, 91, 112

Hodgkinson, Liz, 3–20, 89, 96, 104
holistic care, 26, 37, 40
homoeopathy, 69
honey, 67
hope, 127
hormones, in milk, 9, 65
hospices, 37
Hoxsey clinic, 25
hummus, 70–1
humour, 20
'hurry syndrome', 85
hyperventilation, 80, 84

images, visualisation, 74–9
immune system, 23, 68, 112, 121
Imperial Cancer Research Fund (ICRF), 30, 31, 34, 38–9
Independent, 34
insomnia, 91
Institute of Cancer Research, 39
Iscador, 69
isolation, 126
Issels, Dr Josef, 23–5, 36, 57, 60, 61, 83

Jung, C.G., 49

Kenny, Mary, 34
Kidman, Brenda, 28, 29, 30

The Lancet, 33–6, 38, 42
laughter therapy, 20
LeShan, Lawrence, 10, 54, 106
lentils:
    carrot and lentil soup, 71
libido, 128
liver:
    cancer, 67, 68
    detoxification therapy, 60
London School of Hygiene and Tropical Medicine, 36
low-fat diet, 65

Macausland, Lieutenant-Colonel Marcus, 26, 116
McColl, Ian, 29–31

McElwain, Professor Tim, 29–31, 33, 34, 36, 37
macrobiotic diet, 65
McVie, Professor Gordon, 38
mantras, 112
massage, 18, 87–90
mastectomy, 88, 89, 126
Maxwell-Hudson, Clare, 87–8
meat, 64
meditation, 9, 109–15
meridians, shiatsu, 90–1
Metcalfe, Jane, 45–54, 62–4, 75–6, 81–2, 92–3, 95–6, 97, 99, 101–2, 107, 110
migraine, 91
milk, 60, 65
minerals, 65, 66
    supplements, 9, 68–9
miracle cures, 113
mistletoe, 69
monosodium glutamate, 66
Mount Vernon Hospital, 53
mousse, 73
music, 84
music therapy, 17, 94–6, 99

National Health Service (NHS), 40, 54, 97, 119, 122
natural food, 65
negative thoughts, 78, 113, 114
New Approaches to Cancer, 116
Nixon, Dr Peter, 84, 87
Nowak, Wanda, 70
nutrition *see* Bristol Diet

organic produce, 14, 65
oxygen, 81, 83, 84
ozone, 83

parsnip and cashew bake, 72
Paul, Ann, 29
personal needs, suppression of, 10
personality, 9–10
Pilkington, Canon Christopher, 10, 14, 16, 21–2, 117
Pilkington, Guy, 22

Pilkington, Pat, 12, 14–15, 16, 20, 21–2, 25–9, 32, 41, 57, 116, 124–5
placebo effect, 129
poetry, 99
porridge, rice, 70
potassium, 66, 68
pressure points, 90, 91
prostheses, 88
protein, 64
psycho-oncology, 124, 126, 127–8
psychoneuroimmunology (PNI), 57, 124, 125

quality of life, 127

raw food, 61, 65–6
recipes, 70–3
relaxation, 9, 80–6
rest, 9, 17
rheumatism, 91
rice porridge, 70
Richards, Dr Dick, 29, 30
Ringberg Klinik, Bad Weissee, 24–5, 60, 61
Royal London Homoeopathic Hospital, 35
Royal Marsden Hospital, 38

salt, 60, 61, 66
scars, 88
selenium, 68
self-help groups, 100–4
Seventh Day Adventists, 27, 64
sexuality, 127–8
Shawcross, Jo, 5
Sheard, Tim, 35, 36
shiatsu, 18, 90–1
Siddall, Barbara, 5, 7, 8–9, 13, 16, 17, 19, 20, 82–3
Siddha Yoga, 112
Siegel, Dr Bernie, 129
Sikora, Professor Karol, 35–6, 40, 49–50, 53, 126
Simonton, Carl and Stephanie, 26, 74
singing, 95–6

Sivananda Yoga Centre, 111
sleep, 17
smoking, 13
sodium, 66
Solihull Cancer Support Group, 103
soup, carrot and lentil, 71
soya cream, 73
soya milk, 60
spaghetti vegetariana, 71–2
spiritual healing, 16, 21, 116–18
stimulants, 67–8
stomach cancer, 66
stress, 16, 84, 113
Stuart, Michael, 100–1
sugar, 60, 61, 67
suicide, 79
Sunday Telegraph, 34
supplements, 68–9
support groups, 45, 52, 100–4, 126–7, 128

tea, 67–8
television, 81
Thomson, Dr Rosy see Daniel, Dr Rosy
thoughts, and visualisation, 78
see also emotions
Tiley, Rev. Tim, 116
tiredness, 17
tofu nuggets, 72
touch, 18
massage, 87–90
transcendental meditation (TM), 112

vegan diet, 59, 60
vegetables, 60
vegetarian diet, 59, 60
vinaigrette, 71
visualisation, 26, 74–9, 117
vitamin B complex, 68
vitamin C, 68
vitamin E, 68
vitamins, 65, 66
supplements, 9, 68–9

Walker, Martin J., 36–7   yoga, 82, 84
Weir, Dr Michael, 40, 52
wine, 68   zinc, 68

If you have enjoyed this book, you may also be interested in the following titles also published by Vermilion:

The Eczema Handbook	£7.99
Beat IBS Through Diet	£7.99
Beat PMS Through Diet	£7.99
Beat Sugar Craving	£7.99
The Allergy Survival Guide	£10.99
Evening Primrose Oil	£6.99
Getting Sober and Loving It!	£7.99
Hormone Replacement Therapy	£6.99
How to Stop Smoking	£5.99
The Migraine Handbook	£6.99
The Baldness Cure	£6.99
HypnoHealth	£7.99

To obtain your copy, simply telephone Murlyn Services on 0279 427203

You may pay by cheque/postal order/VISA and should allow 28 days for delivery.